WILLIAMS-SONOMA

Brunch Entertaining

GENERAL EDITOR

Chuck Williams

RECIPES

Janeen Sarlin

PHOTOGRAPHY

Richard Eskite

TIME LIFE BOOKS

TIME-LIFE BOOKS
Time-Life Books is a division of Time Life Inc.
Time-Life is a trademark of Time Warner Inc. U.S.A.

TIME-LIFE CUSTOM PUBLISHING
Vice President and Publisher: Terry Newell
Vice President of Sales and Marketing: Neil Levin
Director of Financial Operations: J. Brian Birky
Director of Acquisitions: Jennifer L. Pearce

WILLIAMS-SONOMA
Founder and Vice-Chairman: Chuck Williams
Book Buyer: Victoria Kalish

WELDON OWEN INC.
President: John Owen
Vice President and Publisher: Wendely Harvey
Chief Operating Officer: Larry Partington
Vice President International Sales: Stuart Laurence
Associate Publisher: Lisa Atwood
Managing Editor: Jan Newberry
Consulting Editor: Norman Kolpas
Copy Editor: Sharon Silva
Design: Kari Perin, Perin+Perin
Production Director: Stephanie Sherman
Production Manager: Jen Dalton
Production Editor: Sarah Lemas
Food Stylist: Pouké
Prop Stylist: Sara Slavin
Photo Production Coordinator: Juliann Harvey
Photo Assistant: Kevin Hossler
Food Styling Assistant: Jeff Tucker
Prop Assistant: Sarah Dawson
Glossary Illustrations: Alice Harth

A NOTE ON WEIGHTS AND MEASURES
All recipes include customary U.S. and metric
measurements. Metric conversions are based on a
standard developed for these books and have been
rounded off. Actual weights may vary.

The Williams-Sonoma Lifestyles Series
conceived and produced by Weldon Owen Inc.
814 Montgomery Street, San Francisco, CA 94133

In collaboration with Williams-Sonoma
3250 Van Ness Avenue, San Francisco, CA 94109

Separations by Colourscan Overseas Co. Pte. Ltd.
Printed in Singapore by Tien Wah Press (Pte.) Ltd.

A WELDON OWEN PRODUCTION
Copyright © 1999 Weldon Owen Inc.
All rights reserved, including the right of
reproduction in whole or in part in any form.

First printed in 1999
10 9 8 7 6 5 4 3 2 1

Library of Congress
Cataloging-in-Publication Data

Sarlin, Janeen
Brunch entertaining / general editor, Chuck Williams;
  recipes by Janeen Sarlin; photography by Richard
  Eskite.
        p. cm. — (Williams-Sonoma lifestyles)
       Includes index.
       ISBN 0-7370-2010-5
    1. Brunches. 2. Entertaining I. Williams,
Chuck. II. Sarlin, Janeen. III. Series.
TX733.S27 1999
641.5'3— dc21   98-35968
                                       CIP

A NOTE ON NUTRITIONAL ANALYSIS
Each recipe is analyzed for significant nutrients per
serving. Not included in the analysis are ingredients
that are optional or added to taste, or are suggested
as an alternative or substitution either in the recipe
or in the recipe introduction or accompanying tip. In
recipes that yield a range of servings, the analysis is
for the middle of that range.

Contents

Welcome

I love sharing brunch with friends late on a weekend morning. Fueled by good food and beverages, the conversation flows freely. It's often the most relaxing time of my week.

To my way of thinking, brunch entertaining and easy entertaining should be synonymous. That's the notion behind the recipes developed by Janeen Sarlin for this volume of the Williams-Sonoma Lifestyles series. Every one has been designed to make the maximum impression with the least amount of kitchen time. The book's introductory text offers the inspiration and information you need to serve a memorable brunch.

Before you start planning your next brunch, however, let me add a few thoughts on how to simplify the task. Once you've chosen your menu (see the suggestions on pages 16–17), take some time to get organized, thinking through and jotting down all the things you'll need to do, including those you can do before the day of your party. There's no reason to be overambitious in your plans. Just a few thoughtfully chosen dishes, successfully cooked and beautifully presented, can make a lasting impression.

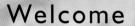

Brunch as an Occasion

A sideboard, a kitchen counter, or a tabletop is readily transformed into a brunch buffet with stacks of individual plates, bundled cutlery and napkins, and an array of serving dishes. To mark each guest's place for a sit-down brunch, attach name tags to small flower pots (below). The pots set a casual tone and provide everyone with a memento of the occasion.

Entertaining Early in the Day

In *The Dictionary of American Food and Drink,* author John Mariani reports that the word *brunch* was coined in Britain in 1895. Joining the words *breakfast* and *lunch,* it described a hearty meal enjoyed by the English gentry after they had returned from an early morning fox hunt. Brunch caught on in the United States in the 1930s and to this day it remains a popular way for people to entertain on weekends.

Almost any event may be celebrated at a brunch, from an engagement to an anniversary, a baby naming to a birthday, a graduation to a homecoming. It is also ideal for nearly any holiday. The casual nature of brunch lends itself to entertaining for no other reason than the desire to get together and share time with family or friends. It is especially well suited to family-style occasions, because the day (usually a Sunday) and the hour (usually in the late morning between eleven and noon) make it easy for guests of all ages to join in the fun.

Brunch, in fact, has become an occasion in its own right. Happening as it does at what is, for a majority of people, the most relaxed time of the week, and featuring the kinds of breakfast and light luncheon foods that many associate with comfort, it epitomizes entertaining in its most casual form.

Choosing a Way to Serve

Of course, brunches are not necessarily casual affairs. When the occasion or the mood calls for it, you can make the meal as formal as you like, setting the table with your finest linens, china, silver, and crystal, and serving food individually plated from the kitchen.

Brunch dishes often lend themselves more readily to a less formal presentation, however. For a small gathering where everyone is seated around a dining table, family-style service is a logical choice. Bring the food out on large platters or in bowls from which guests can help themselves and then easily pass on to the next person.

For larger groups or for the kind of leisurely approach you might want when you have weekend guests, a buffet is a good choice. Select food that's easy for people to eat from plates

that they might well be balancing on their knees. Set up a serving area on a sideboard, complete with hot plates or chafing dishes for keeping hot food hot. Stack plates, bowls, or any other dishes guests might need, along with sets of cutlery bundled inside individual napkins, to one side of the buffet. Then, let guests help themselves. (For more buffet-style serving ideas, see pages 10–11.)

Even the simplest touches can provide a festive mood for the most casual brunch. For example, an attractive tiered pedestal tray (left) puts an assortment of freshly baked sweet breads within easy reach. A hand-woven tray (above) presents brunch beverages in style.

Setting the Scene

The relaxed style of brunch entertaining lends itself to settings both indoors and out. Here, a comfortably weathered porch swing welcomes a guest enjoying Pecan Waffles with Maple Pear Sauce (page 25) and a mug of coffee.

No matter whether you are hosting a formal or informal meal, with food served on individual plates, family style, or as a buffet, the relaxed nature of any brunch allows great flexibility in where and how you choose to present it.

A dining room, of course, is the most obvious site. Most have tables that comfortably seat six to eight guests, whether the meal is formal or casual.

For similarly sized or smaller gatherings, a kitchen large enough to hold a table, or one with an adjoining breakfast room, makes an ideal setting.

Here, the mood is usually even more informal, and the proximity of counters and stove lets willing guests lend a hand in preparing the food.

Brunch entertaining on a larger scale will probably require expanding the dining area beyond these conventional choices. Living or family rooms are logical places, especially if you're serving from a buffet. Rearrange some furniture if necessary to provide guests with seating in groupings that encourage conversation and with tables on which they can rest plates. Make sure, too, that all the seats are comfortable, adding cushions where necessary.

If the weather is nice, you might want to serve your brunch on a patio or in the garden. Set up a buffet either near a door with easy outdoor access or in the open air on a table shaded from sunlight and supplied with mesh domes to keep bugs away from the food. Provide shade for guests by placing tables and chairs—or stretched out blankets on the lawn—under umbrellas, canopies, or shady trees.

Setting the Table and the Mood

Try to set the table the night before you entertain. Then the next morning you'll have more time to prepare the meal and visit with your guests.

Pick dishes that complement the shapes and colors of the foods you'll be serving. (See the photographs throughout this book for examples of such matches.) Simple bouquets of seasonal flowers or baskets or bowls of some of the fresh produce featured in your menu are all that's needed for attractive, easy-to-make centerpieces. To complete the mood, add music suiting a weekend morning and the tastes of your guests, whether classical, jazz, folk, or pop.

Putting Guests at Ease

Remember that the main reason for entertaining is to share a happy occasion with your guests.

Try to think of ways in which you can make your friends feel more at home. Put out the Sunday newspaper for those who might like to browse through it. If you know that some of your guests enjoy cooking, set aside a few last-minute kitchen tasks they might be able to help with.

Whether you plan to serve at the table or from a buffet, consider setting up separate stations where guests can help themselves to breads, cereals, or juices. This is an especially good idea when you are hosting weekend houseguests.

With a juicer and a bowl of citrus fruits, you can turn a kitchen counter into a self-service juice bar (far left). For a casual brunch, let guests help themselves to seasonal fruits (center) and prepare their own toast or cereal (below); you'll make the meal more fun for everyone.

Egg Basics

Whether soft-boiled, poached, scrambled, fried, or made into an omelet, eggs are the quintessential brunch ingredient. For success with two of the most popular egg presentations—filled omelets and the poached eggs featured in Eggs Benedict (page 45)—follow the step-by-step guidelines shown here.

MAKING AN OMELET

1. Melt butter in a nonstick frying pan. Add eggs. As they set, push the edges toward the center, tilting the pan so liquid egg flows underneath.

2. When all the egg has set to a custardlike consistency, arrange the filling, here sautéed mushrooms and shredded cheese, across the center.

3. Shake and tilt the pan to loosen the omelet, making sure that it slides freely. If it sticks to the pan, use the spatula to loosen it.

4. Carefully begin to slide the omelet out of the pan. When it is halfway out, turn your wrist to fold the omelet in half as it leaves the pan.

POACHING EGGS

1. In a wide frying pan, bring water, vinegar, and salt to a boil; reduce the heat to a bare simmer. Break an egg into a small bowl and gently slip it into the water.

2. In the same manner, add the remaining eggs to the simmering water. Cook until the whites are just set and the yolks look glazed but still liquid, about 3 minutes.

3. As each egg is done, lift it from the water with a slotted spoon. Holding it gently on a kitchen towel, trim the edges with kitchen scissors.

BUYING AND STORING EGGS

For the recipes in this book, use large eggs. You can substitute other sizes for cooked egg dishes, but when making batters or doughs, precise measurements are essential to success.

Eggs are also graded AA or A based on shell quality and shape and the white's thickness and clarity. When eggs are to be blended, grade makes little difference. When poached or fried, however, higher-grade eggs will maintain more compact shapes.

When refrigerated, eggs keep for about 4 weeks beyond the "sell by" date. Left at room temperature, eggs will age in a single day the equivalent of one week in the refrigerator.

For recipes that call for raw or partially cooked eggs, consider using pasteurized eggs. These have been heated to a temperature that kills all bacteria without cooking the eggs.

Beverages

Very Berry Smoothies

The secret to a thick and frosty smoothie is to use nearly frozen fruits and juice. Rich in flavor and loaded with vitamins, this restorative drink could be "brunch on the run." If calories matter, substitute nonfat yogurt for the low-fat yogurt and a sugar substitute for the honey. If you like, use 4 perfect blackberries in place of the strawberries for garnish.

1 pint (8 oz/250 g) fresh strawberries, well chilled
1 pint (8 oz/250 g) fresh blueberries, well chilled
1 pint (8 oz/250 g) frozen raspberries, partially thawed
1½ cups (12 oz/375 g) plain low-fat yogurt, well chilled
½ cup (4 fl oz/125 ml) cranberry juice, well chilled
about 2 tablespoons honey or to taste

❀ Set aside 4 perfect strawberries for garnish. Working in batches, in a blender, combine the remaining strawberries, the blueberries, raspberries, yogurt, cranberry juice, and honey. Blend at high speed until smooth, about 3 minutes.

❀ Pour into chilled tall glasses and garnish with the reserved strawberries. Serve at once.

MAKES ABOUT 6 CUPS
(48 FL OZ/1.5 L); SERVES 4

Bloody Marys

Simply omit the vodka to transform this brunch classic into a delicious Virgin Mary.

2½ cups (20 fl oz/625 ml) tomato juice, well chilled
2½ cups (20 fl oz/625 ml) vegetable juice cocktail such as V8 juice or Snappy Tom, well chilled
1½ cups (12 fl oz/375 ml) vodka
¼ cup (2 fl oz/60 ml) lime juice
2 teaspoons Worcestershire sauce
½ teaspoon hot-pepper sauce
salt and ground black pepper to taste
ice cubes
6 celery stalks with leaves

❀ In a pitcher, whisk together the tomato juice, vegetable juice cocktail, vodka, lime juice, and Worcestershire and hot-pepper sauces. Season with salt and black pepper. Taste and adjust the seasonings.

❀ Fill the pitcher with ice cubes and stir well. Strain into glasses and garnish with celery stalks.

MAKES ABOUT 6½ CUPS;
SERVES 6

The Perfect Ramos Fizz

This frothy drink has a taste reminiscent of Key lime pie or lemon-lime sherbet. If using a shaker, make only 1 drink at a time. If using a blender, you can double the recipe with success.

¼ cup (2 fl oz/60 ml) gin
2 teaspoons lemon juice
1 teaspoon lime juice
2 teaspoons sugar
1 egg white (from a pasteurized egg)
2 teaspoons heavy (double) cream
few drops orange-flower water
¾ cup (6 oz/185 g) crushed ice
about ⅓ cup (3 fl oz/80 ml) club soda
ground nutmeg (optional)

✽ In a blender or cocktail shaker, combine the gin, lemon and lime juices, sugar, egg white, cream, orange-flower water, and crushed ice. Blend or vigorously shake until well mixed and frothy, about 1 minute. Pour into a highball glass, fill to the top with club soda, and dust with nutmeg, if using. Serve at once.

SERVES 1

Ginger Lemonade

6½ cups (52 fl oz/1.6 l) water
1 piece fresh ginger, about 3½ oz (105 g), thinly sliced
¾ cup (6 fl oz/180 ml) lemon juice (about 5 lemons)
¾ cup (6 oz/185 g) sugar, or to taste
ice cubes
6 long pineapple sticks, fresh mint sprigs, and/or thin lemon slices, slit to the center

✽ In a nonaluminum saucepan over high heat, bring 4 cups (32 fl oz/1 l) of the water to a boil. Add the ginger, cover, and remove from the heat. Let stand for 5 minutes. Taste and, if a stronger flavor is desired, let stand for 5–10 minutes longer. Pour through a sieve placed over a glass jar, cover, and refrigerate until well chilled.

✽ Pour the lemon juice into a large mixing bowl. Gradually add the sugar, whisking constantly until dissolved. Stir in the remaining 2½ cups (20 fl oz/625 ml) water. Taste and correct the sweetness. Cover and chill well.

✽ Fill a glass pitcher with ice cubes and pour in the ginger tea and the lemonade. Stir well. Pour into chilled glasses. Garnish each glass with a pineapple stick, a mint sprig, and/or a lemon slice.

MAKES ABOUT 7 CUPS
(56 FL OZ/1.75 L); SERVES 6

Planning Menus

The recipes in this book were developed to complement one another, resulting in scores of different menus for brunches small and large, casual and formal. The 10 examples here represent only a handful of the many possible combinations. When planning your brunch menu, keep in mind the character of the recipes: those rich in butter or cheese pair well with those featuring fruit, and a combination of savory and sweet dishes balances the menu.

Summertime Brunch

Very Berry Smoothies
PAGE 14

Crisp Corn Fritters
PAGE 26

Chicken-Apple Sausages

Fresh Melons with
Yogurt Sauce
PAGE 105

Savory Favorites

Bloody Marys
PAGE 14

Stacked Eggs
PAGE 33

Dilled Batter Muffins
PAGE 82

Fresh Fruit

Weekend Guests

Sautéed Apples with Bacon
and Caramelized Onions
PAGE 56

Oatmeal Bran Muffins with
Raisins and Almonds
PAGE 89

Orange Juice

Diner-Style Menu

Nested Eggs

Black and White
Doughnut Holes

Orange Juice

Easter Day Buffet

Ginger Peach–Glazed Ham

Poached Eggs

Cheddar Cheese Buns

Citrus Compote

Elegant Celebration

Champagne

Smoked Salmon
Scrambled Eggs

English Scones

Roasted Figs with
Vanilla Crème Fraîche

Lazy Sunday Morning

Old-fashioned Pecan
Sticky Buns

Spinach and Feta Quiche

Stewed Winter Compote

Coffee or Tea

Al Fresco Gathering

Ginger Lemonade

Crab Cakes with
Avocado Salsa

Honey-Glazed
Baked Peaches

Casual Winter Buffet

Oven-Baked Omelet with
Sausage and Peppers

Sautéed Potatoes

Maple-Glazed Grapefruit

Hearty Weekend Brunch

The Perfect Ramos Fizz

Steak and Eggs

Fresh Strawberry Tart

Stuffed French Toast Grand Marnier

PREP TIME: 40 MINUTES

COOKING TIME: 20 MINUTES

INGREDIENTS

ORANGE WHIPPED BUTTER

½ lb (250 g) unsalted butter, at room
 temperature

grated zest of 1 orange

1 teaspoon Grand Marnier or other
 orange-flavored liqueur

FILLING

¼ cup (1½ oz/45 g) dried cherries

¼ cup (1½ oz/45 g) dried apricots,
 slivered

grated zest of ½ orange

¼ cup (2 fl oz/60 ml) orange juice

2 tablespoons Grand Marnier or
 other orange-flavored liqueur

½ teaspoon ground cinnamon

½ large ripe banana, thinly sliced

12 slices challah bread, each 2 inches
 (5 cm) thick

4 eggs

1 cup (8 fl oz/250 ml) milk

¼ cup (2 fl oz/60 ml) Grand Marnier
 or other orange-flavored liqueur

2 tablespoons light brown sugar

pinch of salt

about 2 tablespoons unsalted butter

Golden French toast stuffed with fresh banana slices and dried cherries and apricots makes a flavorful package that is wonderfully accented by orange-flavored butter. Alternatively, omit the butter and serve with a dusting of confectioners' (icing) sugar.

SERVES 6

❀ To make the orange butter, in a small bowl or a food processor, combine the butter, orange zest, and liqueur and beat or process until smooth. Transfer to individual crocks, if available, and refrigerate until serving.

❀ To make the filling, in a small nonaluminum saucepan over medium heat, combine the cherries, apricots, and orange zest, juice, and liqueur. Bring to a simmer, remove from the heat, stir in the cinnamon, cover, and let stand for 10 minutes. Stir in the banana slices.

❀ Using a small, sharp knife, cut a narrow horizontal slit in the center of one side of each bread slice, keeping three sides intact. Spoon about 1½ tablespoons of the fruit filling into the pocket, then press the top with the palm of your hand to seal. Set aside.

❀ In a shallow bowl, whisk the eggs until frothy. Whisk in the milk, liqueur, brown sugar, and salt. Dip the filled bread slices into the egg mixture and let soak, turning once, for about 2 minutes on each side.

❀ Heat a large, heavy frying pan or griddle over high heat until a few drops of water flicked onto the surface skitter across it. Add about 1 tablespoon of the butter and, when the foam subsides, working in batches, add the French toast. Cook until golden brown on one side, about 3 minutes. Turn and brown the other side, about 2 minutes longer. Keep warm. Repeat until all the French toast is cooked, adding more butter to the pan as needed.

❀ Divide the French toast among warmed individual plates and serve with the orange butter.

NUTRITIONAL ANALYSIS PER SERVING: Calories 458 (Kilojoules 1,924); Protein 16 g; Carbohydrates 60 g; Total Fat 14 g; Saturated Fat 5 g; Cholesterol 267 mg; Sodium 526 mg; Dietary Fiber 2 g

Buttermilk Pancakes with Bing Cherry Syrup

PREP TIME: 20 MINUTES

COOKING TIME: 35 MINUTES

INGREDIENTS

BING CHERRY SYRUP

½ cup (3½ oz/105 g) firmly packed
   brown sugar

½ cup (4 oz/125 g) granulated sugar

1 cup (8 fl oz/250 ml) warm water

1½ cups (9 oz/280 g) stemmed and
   pitted large, ripe Bing cherries

1 teaspoon almond extract (essence)

2 eggs

2 cups (10 oz/315 g) all-purpose
   (plain) flour

2 tablespoons granulated sugar

2 teaspoons baking powder

1 teaspoon baking soda (bicarbonate
   of soda)

1 teaspoon salt

2 cups (16 fl oz/500 ml) buttermilk

¼ cup (2 oz/60 g) unsalted butter,
   melted

½ teaspoon almond extract (essence)

1–2 tablespoons vegetable oil

PREP TIP: To keep the pancakes warm
while you finish cooking all the batter,
transfer them to a rack set over a
baking sheet and put in a 200°F
(95°C) oven, leaving the door slightly
ajar, until ready to serve.

During the early summer months when cherries are in season, look for ripe, juicy Bings. The task of pitting them is easy if you use a cherry pitter, a small utensil found in kitchenware shops.

MAKES TWELVE 6-INCH (15-CM) PANCAKES; SERVES 4

❋ To make the syrup, in a saucepan over high heat, combine the brown and granulated sugars and water and stir until the sugar dissolves. Bring to a boil and cook, uncovered, for 5 minutes. Add the cherries, reduce the heat to low, and simmer until the cherries are cooked, 8–10 minutes. Stir in the almond extract and simmer for about 2 minutes longer to blend the flavors. Remove from the heat and let cool.

❋ In a small bowl, using an electric mixer, beat the eggs until frothy. Add the flour, granulated sugar, baking powder, baking soda, salt, buttermilk, melted butter, and almond extract. Continue to beat just until the mixture is smooth; do not overbeat.

❋ Heat a large, heavy frying pan or griddle over high heat until a few drops of water flicked onto the surface skitter across it. Lightly grease the pan with the vegetable oil (or nonstick cooking spray). Pour about ⅓ cup (3 fl oz/80 ml) of the batter onto the pan. Cook until the surface is covered with tiny bubbles, the batter is set, the bottom is browned, and the edges look dry, about 2 minutes. Flip the pancake over and continue to cook until the second side is golden brown, about 2 minutes longer. Keep warm until all are cooked. Repeat with the remaining batter, adding more oil to the pan as needed.

❋ Serve the pancakes hot, topped with a spoonful of the cherry syrup. Pass the remaining syrup at the table.

NUTRITIONAL ANALYSIS PER SERVING: Calories 770 (Kilojoules 3,234); Protein 15 g; Carbohydrates 130 g; Total Fat 21 g; Saturated Fat 9 g; Cholesterol 142 mg; Sodium 1,315 mg; Dietary Fiber 3 g

Stacked Crepes with Nectarine-Apricot Sauce

PREP TIME: 20 MINUTES,
    PLUS 2 HOURS FOR CHILL-
    ING CREPE BATTER

COOKING TIME: 50 MINUTES

INGREDIENTS

CREPE BATTER

¾ cup (6 fl oz/180 ml) plus 3 table-
    spoons milk

¾ cup (6 fl oz/180 ml) water

3 eggs

1½ cups (7½ oz/235 g) all-purpose
    (plain) flour

pinch of salt

6 tablespoons (3 oz/90 g) unsalted
    butter, melted and cooled

1 teaspoon grated lemon zest

NECTARINE-APRICOT SAUCE

½ lb (250 g) dried apricots

about 2⅔ cups (21 fl oz/660 ml) water

½ cup (4 oz/125 g) granulated sugar

2 tablespoons lemon juice

½ teaspoon grated lemon zest

3 large nectarines, about 1½ lb (750 g),
    halved, pitted, and thinly sliced

½ teaspoon vegetable oil

about ¼ cup (1 oz/30 g) confectioners'
    (icing) sugar

MAKE-AHEAD TIP: The nectarine-apricot sauce can be made up to the point before the nectarine slices are added, then stored up to 2 weeks in advance in the refrigerator.

SERVES 6

❁ To make the crepes, in a bowl, whisk together the milk, water, and eggs until blended. Add the flour and salt all at once and whisk until the batter is completely smooth. Stir in the melted butter and lemon zest. Cover and refrigerate for at least 2 hours or for up to overnight.

❁ Meanwhile, make the sauce: In a saucepan over high heat, combine the apricots, 2 cups (16 fl oz/500 ml) of the water, the granulated sugar, and the lemon juice and bring to a boil, stirring to dissolve the sugar. Reduce the heat to low, cover, and simmer until the apricots are tender, about 35 minutes. Transfer to a food processor or blender and process until smooth. Pour into a measuring pitcher and add the lemon zest and as much of the remaining ⅔ cup (5 fl oz/160 ml) water as needed to measure 3½ cups (28 fl oz/875 ml) total. Just before serving, bring to a simmer over low heat. Set aside a few nectarine slices for garnish and add all the remaining slices to the sauce. Remove from the heat and let stand until the slices are barely tender, about 5 minutes.

❁ To cook the crepes, stir the batter gently and bring to room temperature. Line 2 baking sheets with waxed paper. In a heavy 6-inch (15-cm) crepe pan over high heat, warm the vegetable oil. Pour the oil into a small cup and wipe the pan with a paper towel, leaving only a film. Return the pan to the stove and heat until a few drops of water flicked onto the surface skitter across it. Ladle in about 2 tablespoons batter and immediately swirl the pan to spread it to the edges. Pour off any excess into a separate cup. Cook until the top looks dry and light brown spots appear on the bottom, 1–2 minutes. Flip the crepe and cook until brown spots appear on the second side, about 30 seconds longer. Immediately invert onto the lined baking sheet. Repeat until all the batter is cooked; you should have 25–28 crepes. The first few will not be perfect. Let cool to room temperature.

❁ To assemble: On each of 3 rimmed serving platters, layer about 8 crepes with a generous spoonful of sauce between each layer. Top each stack with about ¼ cup (2 fl oz/60 ml) sauce. Garnish with the reserved nectarine slices and dust with confectioners' sugar. Cut into wedges to serve.

NUTRITIONAL ANALYSIS PER SERVING: Calories 528 (Kilojoules 2,218); Protein 11 g; Carbohydrates 89 g; Total Fat 17 g; Saturated Fat 9 g; Cholesterol 143 mg; Sodium 81 mg; Dietary Fiber 6 g

Pecan Waffles with Maple Pear Sauce

PREP TIME: 30 MINUTES

COOKING TIME: 30 MINUTES

INGREDIENTS

MAPLE PEAR SAUCE

4 firm yet ripe Anjou or Bartlett (Williams') pears, peeled, halved, cored, and cut into slices ¼ inch (6 mm) thick

juice of 1 lemon

¼ cup (2 oz/60 g) unsalted butter

¼ cup (2 fl oz/60 ml) water

grated zest of ½ lemon

1 cup (11 oz/345 g) pure maple syrup, preferably Grade B

½ cup (2 oz/60 g) finely chopped pecans

1¾ cups (9 oz/280 g) all-purpose (plain) flour

1 tablespoon sugar

2 teaspoons baking powder

¼ teaspoon salt

1¾ cups (14 fl oz/430 ml) milk

3 eggs, separated

6 tablespoons (3 oz/90 g) butter, melted and cooled

½ teaspoon vanilla extract (essence)

pinch of cream of tartar

Sifting the dry ingredients and beating the egg whites before adding them to the batter are the secrets to crisp, light waffles. If you're a maple lover, look for the darker Grade B syrup. It has a stronger maple flavor than the more subtle Fancy Grade.

MAKES 6–8 WAFFLES

❀ To make the sauce, place the pear slices in a bowl and toss with the lemon juice. In a large, nonaluminum saucepan over medium heat, melt the butter. Add the pears and sauté gently just to coat with butter, 1–2 minutes. Add the water, lemon zest, and maple syrup, reduce the heat to low, and simmer just until the pears are tender but still hold their shape, about 6 minutes. Using a slotted spoon, transfer the pears to a bowl. Raise the heat to high and reduce the cooking liquid to about 1 cup (8 fl oz/250 ml), about 10 minutes. Pour ½ cup (4 fl oz/125 ml) of the reduced liquid over the pears; reserve the remaining syrup separately. Keep warm or serve at room temperature.

❀ Put the pecans in a small, dry frying pan over medium-low heat and toast, stirring continuously, until fragrant, 2–3 minutes. Remove from the frying pan and set aside.

❀ Preheat a waffle iron following the manufacturer's directions.

❀ In a bowl, sift together the flour, sugar, baking powder, and salt. In a small bowl, whisk together the milk, egg yolks, melted butter, and vanilla. In a third bowl, using an electric mixer, beat together the egg whites and cream of tartar until stiff peaks form. Stir the milk mixture into the dry ingredients, beating until smooth, then stir in the pecans. Finally, gently fold the egg whites into the batter, leaving tiny clouds of whites visible. The batter will look sandy.

❀ Ladle enough batter onto the waffle iron for 1 waffle and immediately close the lid. Cook until all the steaming stops and the iron opens easily, or according to the manufacturer's directions. Using a fork, carefully loosen the waffle from the iron and keep warm until all are cooked or serve at once. Repeat until all the batter is cooked.

❀ To serve, top the waffles with the pear sauce. Pass the reserved syrup at the table.

NUTRITIONAL ANALYSIS PER WAFFLE: Calories 584 (Kilojoules 2,453); Protein 10 g; Carbohydrates 79 g; Total Fat 27 g; Saturated Fat 13 g; Cholesterol 144 mg; Sodium 285 mg; Dietary Fiber 4 g

Crisp Corn Fritters

PREP TIME: 30 MINUTES

COOKING TIME: 25 MINUTES

INGREDIENTS

8 ears of corn

1 or 2 jalapeño chiles, seeded and
minced

1–2 tablespoons chopped fresh
thyme or 1 teaspoon dried thyme

½ teaspoon ground black pepper

½ teaspoon ground white pepper

¼ teaspoon red pepper flakes

4 eggs

1½ cups (12 fl oz/375 ml) milk

1½ cups (7½ oz/235 g) all-purpose
(plain) flour

1 tablespoon granulated sugar

1 teaspoon baking powder

¼ teaspoon salt

about ¼ cup (2 fl oz/60 ml) corn oil

2 tablespoons confectioners' (icing)
sugar, for dusting

These crisp, thyme-laced fritters are a good substitute for bread when serving a frittata or soufflé roll. To serve as part of a brunch main course, arrange thinly sliced baked ham and cheddar cheese on a plate alongside the hot fritters, and pour hot maple syrup over the top.

MAKES 3–4 DOZEN 3-INCH (7.5-CM) FRITTERS

❀ Working with 1 ear of corn at a time, hold the ear by its pointed end, steadying the stalk end in the bottom of a shallow bowl. Using a sharp knife, cut down along the ear to strip off the kernels, turning the ear with each cut. Then run the dull side of the knife blade along the ear, scraping out all of the pulp and milk. Stir in the chiles, thyme, black and white peppers, and red pepper flakes, mixing well.

❀ In another bowl, whisk the eggs until frothy. Whisk in the milk, flour, granulated sugar, baking powder, and salt until well blended. Stir the egg mixture into the corn mixture.

❀ Heat a large, heavy frying pan or griddle over high heat until a few drops of water flicked onto the surface skitter across it. Add about 1 teaspoon of the oil to the pan and, working in batches, drop the batter by tablespoonfuls onto the hot surface. Fry, turning once, until golden brown, about 1 minute on each side. Transfer to paper towels to drain and keep warm. Repeat until all the batter is cooked, adding oil to the pan as needed.

❀ Dust the fritters with the confectioners' sugar, arrange in a pretty napkin-lined platter or basket, and serve at once.

NUTRITIONAL ANALYSIS PER FRITTER: Calories 69 (Kilojoules 290); Protein 2 g; Carbohydrates 10 g; Total Fat 2 g; Saturated Fat 1 g; Cholesterol 21 mg; Sodium 40 mg; Dietary Fiber 1 g

Asparagus and Potato Frittata

PREP TIME: 20 MINUTES

COOKING TIME: 45 MINUTES

INGREDIENTS

¾ lb (375 g) thin asparagus

3–4 tablespoons olive oil

2 large green (spring) onions,
    chopped

6–8 small red potatoes, unpeeled,
    cut into slices ⅛ inch (3 mm) thick

1 teaspoon salt, plus pinch of salt

½ teaspoon chopped fresh tarragon

ground pepper to taste

2 tablespoons snipped fresh chives,
    plus chive blossoms for garnish
    (optional)

3 tablespoons unsalted butter

11 eggs

⅓ cup (1½ oz/45 g) grated Parmesan
    cheese

about ½ cup (2 oz/60 g) shredded
    Swiss cheese

1 bunch watercress, tough stems
    removed

Italian frittatas are made by combining various ingredients with eggs and cooking the mixture on the stove top. Here, the process is simplified by finishing the frittata in the oven.

SERVES 8–10

❀ Cut or snap off the tough ends from the asparagus and place the spears on a steamer rack over boiling water. Cover and steam until tender, about 2 minutes. Remove from the steamer and cut into 1-inch (2.5-cm) lengths. Set aside.

❀ In a large sauté pan over medium heat, warm 3 tablespoons olive oil. Add the onions and sauté until soft and translucent, about 4 minutes. Add the potatoes, 1 teaspoon salt, tarragon, and pepper and sauté until the potatoes glisten, about 3 minutes, adding the remaining 1 tablespoon oil if needed to prevent sticking. Cover and cook until the potatoes are nearly tender, 6–8 minutes. Uncover, raise the heat to high, and cook, stirring constantly, until the potatoes are browned, 7–8 minutes. Stir in the chives and asparagus and remove from the heat.

❀ Preheat an oven to 375°F (190°C).

❀ In a large cast-iron frying pan or ovenproof sauté pan over medium-high heat, melt the butter. Meanwhile, in a bowl, whisk the eggs until blended. Stir in the pinch of salt and the Parmesan cheese and season with pepper. Pour the eggs into the hot pan. Stir gently in the center and, using a fork or spatula, carefully lift the edges and gently push the eggs to one side of the pan, tilting the pan slightly to allow the uncooked egg to flow underneath. Cook until thickened, 3–4 minutes. Spread the vegetables evenly over the eggs. Sprinkle the Swiss cheese on top. Place in the oven and bake until the eggs are set and the cheese melts, about 15 minutes. The cooking time will depend on the size of the pan and whether the vegetables are still hot.

❀ Remove from the oven and let stand for a few minutes, then cut into wedges and serve, garnished with watercress sprigs and chive blossoms, if desired.

NUTRITIONAL ANALYSIS PER SERVING: Calories 278 (Kilojoules 1,168); Protein 13 g; Carbohydrates 15 g; Total Fat 19 g; Saturated Fat 7 g; Cholesterol 280 mg; Sodium 481 mg; Dietary Fiber 2 g

Ham and Cheddar Cheese Gratin

PREP TIME: 20 MINUTES

COOKING TIME: 20 MINUTES

INGREDIENTS

1½ tablespoons unsalted butter

¼ cup (1½ oz/45 g) finely chopped
    yellow onion

1 celery stalk, finely chopped

2⅓ cups (14 oz/440 g) cubed baked
    ham

1 teaspoon chopped fresh tarragon

pinch of ground black pepper

SAUCE

¼ cup (2 oz/60 g) unsalted butter

¼ cup (1½ oz/45 g) all-purpose
    (plain) flour

4 cups (32 fl oz/1 l) milk, heated
    almost to a boil

2 teaspoons chopped fresh tarragon

¼ teaspoon dry mustard

dash of ground nutmeg

dash of cayenne pepper

ground black pepper to taste

¾ cup (4 oz/125 g) finely cubed
    cheddar cheese

6 hard-boiled eggs, peeled

1–2 tablespoons heavy (double)
    cream

¼ cup (1 oz/30 g) shredded cheddar
    cheese

The timeless combination of ham and cheese appears here with the ham in a rich cheddar cheese sauce that also cloaks hard-cooked eggs. Serve with toast points and slices of crisp Granny Smith apple on the side.

SERVES 6

❊ Preheat an oven to 400°F (200°C). Butter a 1½-qt (1½-l) gratin dish or other round or oval shallow baking dish.

❊ In a small sauté pan over medium heat, melt the butter. When the foam subsides, add the onion and celery and sauté until soft and translucent, about 3 minutes. Add the ham and sauté until heated through, about 2 minutes. Mix in the tarragon and season with pepper. Scatter the ham mixture over the bottom of the prepared dish. Set aside.

❊ To make the sauce, in a heavy saucepan over medium-high heat, melt the butter. Add the flour and cook, stirring constantly, for 2 minutes without browning the flour, adjusting the heat as needed. Remove from the heat. Add the hot milk all at once and whisk vigorously to prevent lumps from forming. Return the pan to the heat and cook, stirring constantly, until thickened, about 2 minutes. Season with the tarragon, mustard, nutmeg, cayenne pepper, and black pepper. Stir in the cubed cheese. Taste and adjust the seasonings.

❊ Cut the hard-boiled eggs in half lengthwise; set 6 halves aside. Coarsely chop the remaining halves and stir into the warm sauce. Pour all but about ¼ cup (2 fl oz/60 ml) of the sauce over the ham mixture. Then nest the reserved egg halves, yolk sides up, in the sauce, spacing them evenly so they indicate the center of a serving. Whisk 1–2 tablespoons cream into the reserved sauce to thin it, then spoon over the eggs. Scatter the shredded cheese over the top.

❊ Bake until the sauce is bubbling and the surface is golden brown, 10–12 minutes. Serve directly from the dish.

NUTRITIONAL ANALYSIS PER SERVING: Calories 532 (Kilojoules 2,234); Protein 34 g; Carbohydrates 15 g; Total Fat 37 g; Saturated Fat 20 g; Cholesterol 334 mg; Sodium 1,290 mg; Dietary Fiber 0 g

Stacked Eggs

PREP TIME: 25 MINUTES

COOKING TIME: 50 MINUTES

INGREDIENTS

2 lb (1 kg) sweet or spicy Italian
    sausage, casings removed

1 tablespoon vegetable oil

POTATOES

5 Yukon gold potatoes, about 1½ lb
    (750 g) total weight, peeled

2½ teaspoons coarse salt

1 teaspoon ground white pepper

about ⅓ cup (3 fl oz/80 ml)
    vegetable oil

SPICY TOMATO SAUCE

½ cup (4 fl oz/125 ml) ketchup

1½ tablespoons red pepper flakes

1 teaspoon Worcestershire sauce

½ teaspoon lemon juice

POACHED EGGS

4 qt (4 l) water

3 tablespoons white vinegar

1 tablespoon salt

8 eggs

4–6 fresh parsley sprigs

SERVES 8

❋ Line a baking sheet with a brown paper bag. Divide the sausage into 8 equal portions and shape into patties ½ inch (12 mm) thick. In a large frying pan over high heat, warm the oil. Add the sausage patties and brown, about 3 minutes. Turn and brown on the second side, about 2 minutes longer. Reduce the heat to medium-low, cover partially, and continue cooking until the juices run clear when the patties are pierced with a fork, 10–12 minutes. Transfer to the prepared baking sheet, cover partially with aluminum foil, and keep warm until serving.

❋ To prepare the potatoes, grate them into a bowl. Add the coarse salt and pepper, tossing with a fork to mix.

❋ In a large, heavy frying pan over high heat, warm the oil until it shimmers. Meanwhile, squeeze the shredded potatoes dry between your hands and form into 8 even-sized potato nests. Working quickly, slide each nest into the hot oil and fry until lightly browned on one side, about 10 minutes. Turn the potato nests and continue to fry until crisp and brown on the second side yet tender on the inside, about 10 minutes longer. Transfer to the baking sheet holding the sausage and keep warm until serving.

❋ To make the tomato sauce, in a small bowl, whisk together the ketchup, red pepper flakes, Worcestershire sauce, and lemon juice. Taste and adjust the seasonings. Set aside until serving.

❋ To poach the eggs, in a large sauté pan over high heat, combine the water, vinegar, and salt and bring to a boil. Reduce the heat to just under a boil. One at a time, crack the eggs and slip them into the simmering water. After all the eggs are added, reduce the heat to a gentle simmer. Cook until the whites are just set and the yolks are glazed over but still liquid, about 3 minutes. Using a slotted spoon, transfer the eggs to a kitchen towel to drain. Trim off any streamers of egg white.

❋ To serve, place the potato nests on a serving platter. Top each with a sausage patty, an egg, and a spoonful of sauce. Garnish the platter with the parsley sprigs. Pass the remaining sauce at the table.

NUTRITIONAL ANALYSIS PER SERVING: Calories 435 (Kilojoules 1,827); Protein 27 g; Carbohydrates 21 g; Total Fat 27 g; Saturated Fat 7 g; Cholesterol 288 mg; Sodium 1,398 mg; Dietary Fiber 2 g

Shrimp Gratin

PREP TIME: 35 MINUTES

COOKING TIME: 50 MINUTES

INGREDIENTS

3 lb (1.5 kg) shrimp (prawns),
   peeled and deveined

1 fennel bulb

about 2 tablespoons olive oil

1 small and 1 large yellow onion,
   chopped separately

¼ cup (2 fl oz/60 ml) Pernod or dry
   white wine

3 tablespoons heavy (double) cream

2 tablespoons tomato paste

½ cup (⅔ oz/20 g) chopped fresh dill

¼ cup (⅓ oz/10 g) chopped fresh
   tarragon

¼ cup (⅓ oz/10 g) chopped fresh
   flat-leaf (Italian) parsley

salt and ground black pepper to taste

¼ cup (2 oz/60 g) unsalted butter, plus
   1 tablespoon chilled, cut into bits

½ cup (2½ oz/75 g) all-purpose
   (plain) flour

1½ cups (12 fl oz/375 ml) milk,
   heated almost to a boil

¼ cup (⅓ oz/10 g) chopped fresh dill

pinch of cayenne pepper

6 oz (185 g) Swiss cheese, shredded

1–1⅓ cups (8–11 fl oz/250–330 ml)
   dry white wine or vermouth

½ cup (½ oz/15 g) corn flakes, crushed

This devilishly rich recipe is accented with the delicate aniselike flavors of fresh fennel and Pernod.

SERVES 8

❀ Bring a saucepan three-fourths full of water to a boil over high heat. Add the shrimp and cook just until they curl slightly and are firm to the touch, about 2 minutes. Drain well and set aside.

❀ Cut off the stems, feathery tops, and any bruised outer stalks from the fennel. Thinly slice the bulb crosswise. Set aside.

❀ Preheat an oven to 375°F (190°C). Butter a shallow 4-qt (4-l) baking dish.

❀ In a large sauté pan over medium-high heat, warm the oil. Add the chopped small onion and fennel and sauté until soft and translucent, about 5 minutes. Add the shrimp and sauté for 1 minute. Raise the heat to high, pour in the Pernod or wine, and cook, stirring constantly, until all the liquid evaporates, about 3 minutes. Stir in the cream and tomato paste and cook until bubbly, about 2 minutes. Add the dill, tarragon, and parsley, season with salt and black pepper, and mix well. Transfer to the prepared baking dish and set aside.

❀ In a heavy saucepan over medium heat, melt the ¼ cup (2 oz/60 g) butter. When the foam subsides, add the chopped large onion and sauté until soft and translucent, about 5 minutes. Add the flour, raise the heat to medium-high, and cook, stirring constantly, for 2 minutes without browning the flour, adjusting the heat as needed. Remove from the heat. Add the hot milk all at once and whisk vigorously to prevent lumps from forming. Return the pan to medium heat and cook, stirring constantly, until thickened, about 2 minutes. Season with dill, salt, and cayenne pepper, and add half of the cheese. Stir until the cheese melts. Slowly whisk in the wine or vermouth, adding enough to thin the sauce to a thick and creamy consistency.

❀ Pour the cream sauce evenly over the shrimp mixture, masking it completely. Sprinkle the crushed corn flakes over the surface, then dot with the 1 tablespoon butter. Bake until browned and bubbly, about 30 minutes. Serve hot directly from the dish.

NUTRITIONAL ANALYSIS PER SERVING: Calories 440 (Kilojoules 1,848); Protein 38 g; Carbohydrates 19 g; Total Fat 23 g; Saturated Fat 12 g; Cholesterol 264 mg; Sodium 395 mg; Dietary Fiber 2 g

Nested Eggs

PREP TIME: 30 MINUTES

COOKING TIME: 45 MINUTES

INGREDIENTS

3–4 tablespoons unsalted butter

2 large yellow onions, finely chopped

4 large celery stalks with leaves, finely chopped

2 large baking potatoes, peeled and cubed

2–3 tablespoons olive oil, if needed

½ cup (¾ oz/20 g) chopped fresh flat-leaf (Italian) parsley

1 tablespoon rubbed sage

1 teaspoon dried thyme or 1 table-spoon fresh thyme leaves

salt and ground pepper to taste

about 2 lb (1 kg) cooked turkey, cut into ½-inch (12-mm) cubes (5 heaping cups)

about 1 cup (8 fl oz/250 ml) chicken or turkey broth

12 eggs

SERVING TIP: For individual servings, add the broth and bring to a boil as directed, then divide the turkey mix-ture among 12 buttered ¼-cup (6–fl oz/180-ml) ramekins set on a rimmed baking sheet. Bake, uncovered, for 12 minutes, then make a nest in each ramekin and slip an egg into it. Continue to bake until the eggs are set, 6–8 minutes longer.

Herb-scented turkey hash makes a delicious "nest" in which to bake eggs. This clever dish is an ideal main course for a brunch party held on Thanksgiving weekend, when you're bound to have leftover turkey on hand. If you don't have an ovenproof frying pan large enough to hold 12 eggs, divide the mixture between 2 smaller pans.

SERVES 12

❁ Preheat an oven to 350°F (180°C).

❁ In a heavy, ovenproof frying pan over medium heat, melt the butter. When the foam subsides, add the onions and celery and sauté until they begin to soften, about 4 minutes. Add the potatoes and a little olive oil if needed to prevent sticking, and sauté, stirring often, until lightly browned, about 6 minutes. Add the parsley, sage, thyme, salt, pepper, and turkey and continue cooking, stirring often, until heated through, about 4 minutes. Taste and adjust the seasonings.

❁ Add the broth to the pan and bring to a boil. Transfer the pan to the oven and bake, uncovered, until the potatoes are soft and browned, about 20 minutes. Remove the pan from the oven and, using the back of a tablespoon, make 12 indentations or "nests," in the turkey mixture. Break an egg into each nest. Sprinkle the eggs with salt and pepper. Return the pan to the oven and continue to bake until the eggs are set, 6–8 minutes longer.

❁ To serve, bring the frying pan to the table and transfer the nests to serving plates with a spatula.

NUTRITIONAL ANALYSIS PER SERVING: Calories 299 (Kilojoules 1,256); Protein 30 g; Carbohydrates 10 g; Total Fat 15 g; Saturated Fat 5 g; Cholesterol 280 mg; Sodium 221 mg; Dietary Fiber 1 g

Shiitake Mushroom Omelet

PREP TIME: 20 MINUTES,
PLUS 20 MINUTES FOR
SOAKING MUSHROOMS

COOKING TIME: 15 MINUTES

INGREDIENTS

SHIITAKE MUSHROOM FILLING

1½ teaspoons olive oil

1 large shallot, chopped

4 small fresh shiitake mushrooms, brushed clean, stems removed, and thinly sliced

4 dried shiitake mushrooms, soaked in warm water to soften for 20 minutes, drained, squeezed dry, stems removed, and thinly sliced

1 tablespoon Madeira wine

salt and ground pepper to taste

3½–4 oz (105–125 g) Gruyère or Comté cheese, shredded

12 eggs

2 tablespoons water

freshly ground pepper to taste

4 tablespoons (2 oz/60 g) plus 2 teaspoons unsalted butter

MAKE-AHEAD TIP: The filling can be made, covered, and refrigerated for up to 5 days or frozen for up to 1 month before serving. Bring to room temperature before cooking the omelets.

The secret to making a good omelet is to add water, not milk or cream, to the beaten eggs and to have the butter just beginning to brown—but not burning—when you add the eggs to the pan. Garnish the omelet with radish sprouts, if you like.

SERVES 4

❋ To make the filling, in a small sauté pan over medium-high heat, warm the olive oil. Add the shallot and sauté until it begins to soften, about 2 minutes. Add the fresh and dried mushrooms, raise the heat to high, and sauté, stirring constantly, until beginning to brown, about 5 minutes. Stir in the Madeira and cook until all the liquid evaporates, about 2 minutes. Season with salt and pepper. Remove from the heat.

❋ Preheat an oven to 200°F (95°C). Place the mushrooms and the cheese near the stove. In a small bowl, using a fork, beat together 3 of the eggs, 1½ teaspoons of the water, and a grinding of fresh pepper just until blended.

❋ In a nonstick 6- to 7-inch (15- to 18-cm) omelet pan over medium heat, melt 1 tablespoon of the butter. When the butter begins to brown, pour in the eggs. Immediately shake the pan back and forth while tilting it and cook until the eggs begin to thicken, about 15 seconds. Spoon about 1½ tablespoons mushroom filling in the center of the omelet, sprinkle with one-fourth of the cheese, and cook for about 10 seconds. Using a fork or spatula, carefully lift the edges and gently push the eggs to one side of the pan, tilting the pan slightly to allow the uncooked egg to flow underneath. Then fold the omelet in half, pressing down firmly to solidify the eggs, and let cook for about 10 seconds longer.

❋ Turn the omelet out onto a baking sheet and keep warm in the oven. Repeat with the remaining eggs, filling, and cheese, adding 1 tablespoon butter to the pan before cooking each omelet, to make a total of 4 omelets. Transfer the omelets to warmed individual plates.

❋ Add the remaining 2 teaspoons butter to the omelet pan, melt over medium heat, and then let brown for about 10 seconds. Drizzle evenly over the omelets and serve at once.

NUTRITIONAL ANALYSIS PER SERVING: Calories 490 (Kilojoules 2,058); Protein 28 g; Carbohydrates 6 g; Total Fat 39 g; Saturated Fat 18 g; Cholesterol 703 mg; Sodium 281 mg; Dietary Fiber 1 g

Crab Cakes with Avocado Salsa

PREP TIME: 25 MINUTES, PLUS
3 HOURS FOR CHILLING

COOKING TIME: 20 MINUTES

INGREDIENTS

2 lb (1 kg) cooked lump crabmeat, picked over for shell fragments and flaked

½ cup (1½ oz/45 g) minced green (spring) onions, including tender green tops

½ cup (4 oz/125 g) minced pimiento

½ cup (4 fl oz/125 ml) mayonnaise

3 egg yolks, lightly beaten

1 tablespoon minced jalapeño chile, or to taste

½ teaspoon cayenne pepper

salt and ground black pepper to taste

2 cups (4 oz/120 g) fresh bread crumbs

about ⅓ cup (3 fl oz/80 ml) vegetable oil for frying

AVOCADO SALSA

1 large Haas avocado, halved, pitted, peeled, and cut into ¼-inch (6-mm) dice

1 small red (Spanish) onion, minced

1 tablespoon chopped fresh tarragon

1 tablespoon chopped fresh chervil

2 tablespoons lime juice, or to taste

1 teaspoon salt

ground black pepper to taste

Jalapeño and cayenne season these fabulous crab cakes served with an herb-laced avocado salsa. Only a small amount of bread crumbs is mixed into the crab cake mixture, so don't skip the chilling time or the cakes will fall apart when cooked.

SERVES 8

❋ In a bowl, combine the crabmeat, green onions, pimiento, mayonnaise, egg yolks, jalapeño chile, and cayenne pepper, and season with salt and black pepper. Mix well. Add ½ cup (1 oz/30 g) of the bread crumbs and mix again. Fry about 1 tablespoon of the mixture in a little oil in a small sauté pan, then taste and adjust the seasonings. Place the remaining 1½ cups (3 oz/90 g) crumbs on a plate. Line a baking sheet with plastic wrap.

❋ Form the crab mixture into 8 cakes each ½ inch (12 mm) thick. Coat each cake in the bread crumbs, place on the lined baking sheet, cover with plastic wrap, and chill in the refrigerator until firm, at least 3 hours or for up to 6 hours.

❋ Meanwhile, make the salsa: In a bowl, combine the avocado, onion, tarragon, chervil, and 2 tablespoons lime juice. Stir together with a fork, then season with salt, black pepper, and more lime juice, if necessary. Cover with plastic wrap pressed directly on top and refrigerate until serving.

❋ Just before serving, in a large sauté pan over medium-high heat, warm the vegetable oil. Working in batches, add the crab cakes and sauté, turning once, until golden brown on both sides, about 4 minutes on each side. Transfer to paper towels to drain for about 2 minutes.

❋ Serve on warmed individual plates. Pass the salsa at the table.

NUTRITIONAL ANALYSIS PER SERVING: Calories 399 (Kilojoules 1,676); Protein 27 g; Carbohydrates 13 g; Total Fat 27 g; Saturated Fat 4 g; Cholesterol 202 mg; Sodium 767 mg; Dietary Fiber 1 g

Oven-Baked Omelet with Sausage and Peppers

PREP TIME: 30 MINUTES

COOKING TIME: 1¾ HOURS

INGREDIENTS

SAUSAGE FILLING

10 oz (315 g) Italian sausages,
    a mixture of sweet and hot

½ head garlic, unpeeled, plus 4 cloves

1½ cups (12 fl oz/375 ml) red wine

2 tablespoons olive oil

1 leek, about 1½ inches (4 cm) in
    diameter, white part only, julienned

½ red bell pepper (capsicum), seeded
    and cut lengthwise into strips

½ yellow bell pepper (capsicum),
    seeded and cut lengthwise into
    strips

1 green bell pepper (capsicum),
    seeded and cut lengthwise into
    strips

1 teaspoon minced fresh oregano

salt and ground black pepper to taste

5–6 tablespoons (2½–3 oz/75–90 g)
    unsalted butter

9 eggs, separated

pinch of salt

¼ cup (1½ oz/45 g) all-purpose
    (plain) flour

½ cup (4 fl oz/125 ml) heavy (double)
    cream or half-and-half (half cream)

pinch of cayenne pepper

ground black pepper to taste

½ cup (2 oz/60 g) grated Parmesan
    cheese

When you want to serve omelets, but don't want to cook them individually, this recipe is ideal. Serve with fresh tomato salsa.

SERVES 6

❈ To make the filling, in a large nonaluminum saucepan over medium-high heat, combine the sausages and ½ head garlic with enough cold water to cover by 1 inch (2.5 cm). Cover, bring to a boil, reduce the heat to low, and simmer until the fat spurts out when the sausages are pierced with a fork, about 25 minutes. Drain the sausages, cut into slices ¼ inch (6 mm) thick, and return to a clean pan. Add the 4 cloves garlic and the red wine. Bring to a boil, reduce the heat to low, cover partially, and cook until the wine is absorbed, about 45 minutes. Remove from the heat.

❈ In a large sauté pan over medium-high heat, warm the olive oil. Add the leek and sauté until beginning to soften, about 5 minutes. Stir in the bell peppers and continue to sauté until the vegetables are tender, about 10 minutes. Season with the oregano, salt, and black pepper. Add the sausage, stir to mix well, taste, and adjust the seasonings.

❈ Preheat an oven to 400°F (200°C).

❈ Place the butter in a 10-inch (25-cm) baking dish and put it into the oven until the butter melts and becomes nutty brown, about 5 minutes.

❈ Meanwhile, in a bowl, using an electric mixer, beat together the egg whites and pinch of salt until stiff peaks form. In another bowl, beat the egg yolks until thick. Add the flour, cream, cayenne, and black pepper to the yolks and mix well. Gently fold in the whites.

❈ Remove the dish from the oven. Pour half of the egg mixture into the hot dish, scatter on the sausage filling, then top with the remaining egg mixture, sprinkle with the Parmesan cheese, and return the dish to the oven. Bake for 5 minutes. Reduce the oven temperature to 350°F (180°C) and continue to bake until light brown on top and firm when pressed with a finger, 15–17 minutes.

❈ Cut the omelet into wedges and serve directly from the dish.

NUTRITIONAL ANALYSIS PER SERVING: Calories 629 (Kilojoules 2,642); Protein 25 g; Carbohydrates 40 g; Total Fat 42 g; Saturated Fat 19 g; Cholesterol 408 mg; Sodium 641 mg; Dietary Fiber 3 g

Eggs Benedict

PREP TIME: 20 MINUTES

COOKING TIME: 15 MINUTES

INGREDIENTS

HOLLANDAISE SAUCE

4 egg yolks

3½ tablespoons lemon and lime juice

1 tablespoon water

⅛ teaspoon salt

2 pinches of ground white pepper

pinch of cayenne pepper

1 cup (8 oz/250 g) unsalted butter, melted and allowed to cool slightly

4 English muffins, split, or 8 crumpets

1 tablespoon unsalted butter

8 slices baked ham, each ¼ inch (6 mm) thick and cut to fit the muffins or crumpets

4 qt (4 l) water

⅓ cup (3 fl oz/80 ml) distilled white vinegar

1 tablespoon salt

8 eggs

MAKE-AHEAD TIP: To poach the eggs in advance, cook as directed, but remove from the water after about 2 minutes and slip into ice water to halt the cooking. Refrigerate in fresh ice water for up to 12 hours, then reheat in a sieve lowered into simmering water for 30 seconds.

This well-known brunch dish never goes out of style. When tomatoes are in season, consider topping the ham with a broiled tomato slice before crowning it with the egg and the hollandaise.

SERVES 8

❀ Preheat a broiler (griller).

❀ To make the sauce, in a small, heavy saucepan over very low heat, combine the egg yolks, lemon and lime juice, and water. Whisk constantly until the mixture just begins to thicken. Continue whisking for 1 minute, but remove the pan from the heat as soon as the mixture thickens. Scrape into a blender, add the salt and the white and cayenne peppers, and blend until smooth. Let cool for 1 minute. With the motor running, slowly pour in the melted butter in a thin stream until all of it has been incorporated. Taste and adjust the seasonings. Pour into a bowl and place over (not touching) hot water in a saucepan.

❀ Lightly spread the cut sides of the muffins or the crumpets with 2 teaspoons of the butter and place on a broiler pan. Broil (grill) until brown, about 6 minutes. Turn off the broiler, cover the muffins with aluminum foil, and keep warm in the oven.

❀ Meanwhile, in a small sauté pan over medium-high heat, melt the remaining 1 teaspoon butter. Add the ham and cook, turning once, until sizzling and beginning to brown, about 4 minutes total. Transfer to a baking sheet and keep warm in the oven.

❀ In a large sauté pan over high heat, combine the water, vinegar, and salt and bring to a boil. Reduce the heat to just under a boil. One at a time, crack the eggs and slip them into the simmering water. After all the eggs are added, reduce the heat to a gentle simmer. Cook until the whites are just set and the yolks are glazed over but still liquid, about 3 minutes. Using a slotted spoon, transfer the eggs to a kitchen towel to drain. Trim off any streamers of egg white.

❀ Place a muffin half or a crumpet on each warmed individual plate. Top with a slice of ham and then an egg. Divide the sauce evenly among the servings, spooning it over the tops. Serve at once.

NUTRITIONAL ANALYSIS PER SERVING: Calories 439 (Kilojoules 1,844); Protein 16 g; Carbohydrates 14 g; Total Fat 35 g; Saturated Fat 18 g; Cholesterol 402 mg; Sodium 810 mg; Dietary Fiber 0 g

Spinach and Feta Quiche

PREP TIME: 25 MINUTES, PLUS
1½ HOURS FOR CHILLING

COOKING TIME: 55 MINUTES

INGREDIENTS

PASTRY

3 cups (15 oz/470 g) all-purpose
(plain) flour

½ teaspoon salt

1 cup (8 oz/250 g) chilled unsalted
butter, cut into small pieces

1 egg

6–8 tablespoons (3–4 fl oz/90–125 ml)
ice water

¾ cup (3 oz/90 g) shredded Swiss
cheese

SPINACH FILLING

2 packages (10 oz/315 g each) frozen
chopped spinach, thawed

1 tablespoon unsalted butter

2 tablespoons olive oil

¼ cup (1½ oz/45 g) finely chopped
yellow onion

10 green (spring) onions, chopped

1 clove garlic, minced

⅔ cup (1 oz/30 g) chopped fresh dill

1 teaspoon ground pepper

3 eggs

1 cup (8 fl oz/250 ml) half-and-half
(half cream)

½ cup (4 fl oz/125 ml) heavy (double)
cream

¼ lb (125 g) feta cheese

¼ cup (1½ oz/45 g) pitted Kalamata
olives, chopped

SERVES 6

❀ To make the pastry, in a bowl, stir together the flour and salt. Add the butter and, using a pastry blender, cut it in until the mixture resembles coarse meal. In a small bowl, using a fork, beat the egg with 2 tablespoons of the ice water. Make a well in the flour mixture and pour in the egg mixture and 2 more tablespoons ice water. Using the fork, mix lightly, adding more ice water as needed until the mixture holds together. Pat into a ball, wrap in plastic wrap, and refrigerate for 1 hour.

❀ On a floured work surface, roll out the pastry into a round about 13 inches (33 cm) in diameter. Transfer to an 11-inch (28-cm) tart pan with a removable bottom, turn under the edges to make them flush with the pan rim, and prick the bottom in several places with a fork. Press a piece of aluminum foil, shiny side down, onto the crust, and freeze for about 30 minutes. Preheat an oven to 425°F (220°C).

❀ Bake the foil-lined pastry shell for 8 minutes. Remove the foil and continue baking until the crust looks dull, about 4 minutes longer. Remove from the oven, sprinkle with the Swiss cheese, and reduce the oven temperature to 375°F (190°C).

❀ Meanwhile, make the filling: Drain the spinach and squeeze dry. In a large sauté pan over medium heat, melt the butter with the oil. Add the yellow and green onions and garlic and sauté until soft, about 4 minutes. Add the spinach and sauté, stirring, until completely wilted, about 3 minutes. Add the dill and pepper and continue sautéing for about 2 minutes longer. Taste and adjust the seasonings; the mixture should taste peppery. Let cool for 5–6 minutes.

❀ In a pitcher or bowl, whisk the eggs until blended, then whisk in the half-and-half and cream. Crumble the feta cheese into the spinach and stir in the cream mixture. Pour into the prebaked shell.

❀ Bake until the filling is puffed and light brown and a knife inserted into the center comes out clean, 35–40 minutes. Remove from the oven and let stand for 5–10 minutes. Garnish with the olives and serve.

NUTRITIONAL ANALYSIS PER SERVING: Calories 922 (Kilojoules 3,872); Protein 24 g; Carbohydrates 67 g; Total Fat 63 g; Saturated Fat 35 g; Cholesterol 301 mg; Sodium 718 mg; Dietary Fiber 5 g

Confetti Crabmeat Soufflé Roll

PREP TIME: 40 MINUTES

COOKING TIME: 35 MINUTES

INGREDIENTS

CRABMEAT FILLING

2 tablespoons unsalted butter

8 green (spring) onions, including 2 inches (5 cm) of the green tops, finely chopped

¼ cup (1½ oz/45 g) minced fresh green chiles

¼ cup (1½ oz/45 g) minced red bell pepper (capsicum)

1 lb (500 g) cooked lump crabmeat, picked over for shells and flaked

⅓ cup (½ oz/15 g) chopped fresh dill

1 tablespoon lemon juice

½ lb (250 g) cream cheese, at room temperature

about 1½ tablespoons heavy (double) cream

salt and ground black pepper to taste

SOUFFLÉ ROLL

¼ cup (2 oz/60 g) unsalted butter

½ cup (2½ oz/75 g) all-purpose (plain) flour

1 teaspoon salt, plus pinch of salt

2 cups (16 fl oz/500 ml) milk, heated almost to a boil

¼ teaspoon ground white pepper

pinch of cayenne pepper

5 eggs, separated

6 tablespoons (1½ oz/45 g) grated Parmesan cheese

fresh chives, snipped

SERVES 12

❀ To make the filling, in a small sauté pan over medium heat, melt the butter. Add the onions, chiles, and bell pepper and sauté until soft, about 3 minutes. Stir in the crabmeat and sauté until heated through, about 3 minutes. Stir in the dill and lemon juice and remove from the heat. In a bowl, whisk together the cream cheese and enough cream to create a smooth, creamy mixture. Stir in the crabmeat mixture and season with salt and black pepper. Cover and set aside.

❀ Preheat an oven to 400°F (200°C). Butter a 15½-by-10½-by-1-inch (39-by-26.5-by-2.5-cm) jelly-roll (Swiss roll) pan. Line with parchment (baking) paper, butter the paper, dust with flour, and tap out the excess.

❀ To make the soufflé roll, in a saucepan over medium-high heat, melt the butter and stir in the flour and 1 teaspoon salt. Cook, stirring, until blended, 2–3 minutes; do not brown. Remove from the heat and add the milk all at once, whisking to remove lumps. Return to medium-high heat, bring to a boil, reduce the heat to medium, and cook, stirring, for 1 minute. Remove from the heat and stir in the white and cayenne peppers.

❀ In a small bowl, whisk the egg yolks until blended. Slowly whisk in about 1 cup (8 fl oz/250 ml) of the hot sauce, then whisk into the sauce until no yellow streaks remain. Set over medium heat and cook, stirring, for 1 minute. Do not allow to boil. Remove from the heat.

❀ In a bowl, beat together the egg whites and a pinch of salt until stiff peaks form. Carefully fold the whites into the warm sauce until incorporated. Immediately spread the mixture in the prepared pan.

❀ Bake until puffed and brown and the center springs back when lightly pressed, 25–30 minutes.

❀ Meanwhile, lay a kitchen towel on a large cake rack and sprinkle evenly with 4 tablespoons of the Parmesan cheese. When the soufflé is done, immediately invert the pan onto the prepared towel. Lift off the pan and peel off the paper. Using a rubber spatula, spread the filling evenly on the soufflé. Using the towel and starting from a long side, roll up the soufflé. Using the towel as a cradle, transfer the roll, seam side down, to a serving platter. Sprinkle with the remaining 2 tablespoons cheese and garnish with the chives. Serve hot or at room temperature, cut into slices.

NUTRITIONAL ANALYSIS PER SERVING: Calories 267 (Kilojoules 1,121); Protein 16 g; Carbohydrates 9 g; Total Fat 19 g; Saturated Fat 11 g; Cholesterol 175 mg; Sodium 484 mg; Dietary Fiber 1 g

Steak and Eggs

PREP TIME: 30 MINUTES

COOKING TIME: 1 HOUR

INGREDIENTS

CARAMELIZED ONIONS

3 heads garlic, unpeeled and cloves
   separated

½ cup (4 fl oz/125 ml) chicken broth

10 tablespoons (5 fl oz/160 ml)
   olive oil

8 large red (Spanish) onions, thinly
   sliced

salt and ground black pepper to taste

4 tablespoons (2 oz/60 g) brown
   sugar

2 tablespoons balsamic vinegar

cayenne pepper to taste

6 New York strip steaks, each about
   ½ lb (250 g) and 1 inch (2.5 cm)
   thick, trimmed of excess fat

about 1 teaspoon coarsely ground
   black pepper

pinch of coarse salt

2½ tablespoons unsalted butter

6 eggs

salt and ground black pepper to taste

Guests with hearty appetites will love this satisfying dish. Cook up a batch of Sautéed Potatoes (page 60) and have the makings for Bloody Marys (page 14) on hand.

SERVES 6

❀ To make the caramelized onions, preheat an oven to 375°F (190°C). In a small baking dish, place the garlic and broth. Drizzle about 2 tablespoons of the olive oil over the top. Cover and bake until the garlic is soft, about 35 minutes. Let cool, covered, for 10 minutes, then uncover, let cool, peel, and slice the garlic; set aside.

❀ Meanwhile, brush 2 large rimmed baking sheets with 2 tablespoons of the olive oil each. Divide the onions evenly between the prepared baking sheets and season with salt and black pepper. Sprinkle 1½ tablespoons of the brown sugar evenly over all the onions, then drizzle about 2 tablespoons oil over each pan. Bake, stirring every 15 minutes, until golden brown, about 45 minutes. Remove from the oven and stir in the garlic. In a small bowl, stir together the vinegar, cayenne pepper, and the remaining 2½ tablespoons brown sugar, then drizzle evenly over all the onions. Return to the oven and bake until evenly browned and caramelized, about 20 minutes longer. Transfer to a bowl, taste, and adjust the seasonings; keep warm.

❀ While the onions cook, score the edges of the steaks every inch (2.5 cm) or so. Rub the coarse black pepper on both sides and let stand for 5–10 minutes. Then, place a large, well-seasoned cast-iron or nonstick frying pan over high heat and sprinkle with the coarse salt. When very hot, add the steaks and sear, turning once, until browned on both sides, about 2 minutes on each side for rare, or until done to your liking.

❀ Meanwhile, in a nonstick sauté pan over medium heat, melt the butter. Break the eggs into the pan, reduce the heat to low, cover, and cook until the whites are set and the yolks are glazed but still liquid, 3–5 minutes, or until done as desired. Season with salt and black pepper.

❀ Transfer the steaks to warmed individual plates and place the eggs alongside. Spoon a generous serving of the caramelized onions between the steak and eggs and serve.

NUTRITIONAL ANALYSIS PER SERVING: Calories 916 (Kilojoules 3,847); Protein 68 g; Carbohydrates 46 g; Total Fat 52 g; Saturated Fat 14 g; Cholesterol 394 mg; Sodium 333 mg; Dietary Fiber 5 g

Smoked Salmon Scrambled Eggs

PREP TIME: 10 MINUTES

COOKING TIME: 12 MINUTES

INGREDIENTS

4–5 tablespoons (2–2½ oz/60–75 g) unsalted butter

4 green (spring) onions, white part and about 2 inches (5 cm) of the green tops, chopped

8 eggs

¼–½ teaspoon ground pepper

3 oz (90 g) smoked salmon, chopped

3 oz (90 g) cream cheese, cut into ¼-inch (6-mm) cubes, at room temperature

fresh tarragon sprigs (optional)

Keeping the heat low and using only butter (no milk, please) create creamy, soft, buttery scrambled eggs. Serve with toasted bagels for brunch, or add asparagus and open a bottle of champagne for a late-night supper.

SERVES 4

❀ In a large, heavy nonstick sauté pan over low heat, melt the butter. Set aside 2 tablespoons of the green onions to use for garnish, and add the remaining green onions to the pan. Sauté until soft and translucent, about 3 minutes. Meanwhile, in a bowl, using a fork, beat the eggs with pepper to taste until blended. Pour the eggs into the sauté pan and, using a wooden spoon, continuously stir, reaching the bottom and edges of the pan, until the eggs begin to thicken and break into curds, about 5 minutes. Keep stirring until the eggs are almost firm, about 4 minutes longer.

❀ Remove from the heat and fold the salmon and cream cheese into the eggs. Return to low heat for about 30 seconds to melt the cheese. Transfer to warmed plates or a platter, sprinkle with the reserved green onions, and garnish with tarragon sprigs, if you like. Serve at once.

NUTRITIONAL ANALYSIS PER SERVING: Calories 368 (Kilojoules 1,546); Protein 18 g; Carbohydrates 3 g; Total Fat 31 g; Saturated Fat 16 g; Cholesterol 488 mg; Sodium 618 mg; Dietary Fiber 0 g

Ginger Peach–Glazed Ham

PREP TIME: 20 MINUTES

COOKING TIME: 3½ HOURS,
   PLUS 25 MINUTES FOR
   RESTING

INGREDIENTS

5 cinnamon sticks, each about
   6 inches (15 cm) long

1 precooked smoked ham, about
   15 lb (7.5 kg)

2 cups (16 fl oz/500 ml) dry white
   wine

GLAZE

1 jar (15 oz/470 g) peach preserves

1 tablespoon minced pickled ginger

1½ teaspoons ground dry ginger

1 teaspoon dry mustard

4 tablespoons (2 oz/60 g) firmly
   packed light brown sugar

1 head chicory (curly endive),
   separated into leaves

MAKE-AHEAD TIP: The ham can be
baked, cooled, covered with plastic
wrap, and refrigerated for up to 3 days.
Allow time in your schedule for the
ham to come to room temperature
before serving.

The ham tastes great hot and even better served at room temperature, when the cinnamon flavor is more pronounced. For the best flavor, look for peach preserves made with just fruit and sugar, and no artificial ingredients.

SERVES 20–24

❊ Preheat an oven to 325°F (165°C).

❊ Break the cinnamon sticks into 1½–2-inch (4–5-cm) pieces. Using a sharp knife, cut 8 or 9 horizontal slits, each ⅛–¼ inch (3–6 mm) deep and running at an angle in the upper, more fatty side of the ham. Slip the cinnamon-stick pieces into the slits, poking them into the meat.

❊ Set the ham on a rack in a large roasting pan, cinnamon side up. Pour the wine into the bottom of the pan and tent the ham with aluminum foil, sealing the edges securely. Bake for 2 hours.

❊ Meanwhile, in a small saucepan over medium heat, combine the peach preserves, pickled ginger, dry ginger, and mustard. Stir well and heat until the preserves melt, forming a glaze.

❊ After 2 hours, remove the ham from the oven and poke any loose cinnamon sticks back into the meat. Raise the oven temperature to 350°F (180°C). Stir about 2 tablespoons of the pan juices into the glaze to thin slightly. Then spoon about three-fourths of the glaze over the top of the ham. Sprinkle 2 tablespoons of the brown sugar on top of the peach glaze, then pat it with the back of a spoon so that it clings to the meat. Return the ham to the oven and continue baking for 1 hour. After the hour, baste with the pan juices and spoon the remaining glaze over the top. Pat with the remaining sugar. Continue to bake until the glaze is browned and bubbly and an instant-read thermometer inserted into the thickest part of the ham registers 140°F (60°C), about 30 minutes longer. Remove from the oven, tent loosely with foil, and let rest for 25 minutes before carving.

❊ Transfer the ham to a large platter and garnish with the chicory. Beginning at the large end of the ham, carve across the grain into thin slices and arrange them around the platter. Serve hot or at room temperature.

NUTRITIONAL ANALYSIS PER SERVING: Calories 139 (Kilojoules 584); Protein 17 g; Carbohydrates 8 g; Total Fat 4 g; Saturated Fat 1 g; Cholesterol 40 mg; Sodium 1,222 mg; Dietary Fiber 0 g

Sautéed Apples with Bacon and Caramelized Onions

PREP TIME: 15 MINUTES

COOKING TIME: 25 MINUTES

INGREDIENTS

I teaspoon unsalted butter

I tablespoon olive oil

1½ lb (750 g) Canadian bacon, thinly sliced

4 large yellow onions, sliced

4 large tart, red apples such as Macoun or Jonathan, cored and cut crosswise into rings ½ inch (12 mm) thick, plus I apple, cored and thinly sliced lengthwise

ground pepper to taste

This simple combination of apples, onions, and bacon is an excellent quick dish to serve to houseguests. Serve with buttered black bread.

SERVES 8

❊ In a large, heavy sauté pan over medium-high heat, melt the butter with the oil. When the foam subsides, add the bacon and sauté until lightly browned and crisp, 5–10 minutes. Using tongs or a slotted spoon, transfer to paper towels to drain; set aside.

❊ In the same pan over medium heat, sauté the onions in the fat remaining in the pan until soft and translucent, about 8 minutes. Add the apple rings and cover the pan. Reduce the heat to low and cook, shaking the pan gently, until the apples are nearly soft but still keep their shape, about 6 minutes. Return the bacon to the pan, cover, and cook until the bacon is hot, about 4 minutes. Season generously with pepper.

❊ Transfer to a warmed platter and garnish with the thin apple slices. Serve at once.

NUTRITIONAL ANALYSIS PER SERVING: Calories 257 (Kilojoules 1,079); Protein 19 g; Carbohydrates 27 g; Total Fat 9 g; Saturated Fat 2 g; Cholesterol 44 mg; Sodium 1,203 mg; Dietary Fiber 4 g

Roast Beef Hash

PREP TIME: 35 MINUTES

COOKING TIME: 45 MINUTES

INGREDIENTS

3 tablespoons unsalted butter

3 large yellow onions, chopped

3 large baking potatoes, peeled and chopped

2–3 tablespoons vegetable oil, if needed

about 2½ lb (1.25 kg) cooked roast beef, cut into large cubes (5 heaping cups)

¼ cup (⅓ oz/10 g) chopped fresh flat-leaf (Italian) parsley

1 tablespoon chopped fresh rosemary leaves

1 tablespoon chopped fresh marjoram leaves

salt and ground pepper to taste

1 cup (8 fl oz/250 ml) milk

fresh flat-leaf (Italian) parsley, chopped, for garnish

The combination of marjoram and rosemary lends an herbal note to this classic breakfast dish. While it bakes unattended in the oven, you're free to visit with your guests. Top each portion with a fried or poached egg, if you like. For instructions on poaching, see page 13.

SERVES 6

❀ Preheat an oven to 375°F (190°C).

❀ In a heavy, ovenproof frying pan, preferably cast iron, melt the butter over medium heat. When the foam subsides, add the onions and sauté until they begin to soften, about 3 minutes. Add the potatoes (and the oil if needed to prevent sticking) and fry, turning often with a spatula, until browned, about 8 minutes. Add the roast beef and fry, stirring often, until lightly browned, 3–4 minutes. Add the ¼ cup (⅓ oz/10 g) parsley, rosemary, and marjoram and season with salt and pepper. Mix well, taste, and adjust the seasonings. Pour in the milk and bring to a boil.

❀ Transfer the pan to the oven and bake, uncovered, until the potatoes are browned and tender, about 30 minutes. Serve hot, directly from the pan, or transfer to a warmed serving dish, and sprinkle with the parsley.

NUTRITIONAL ANALYSIS PER SERVING: Calories 688 (Kilojoules 2,890); Protein 55 g; Carbohydrates 27 g; Total Fat 39 g; Saturated Fat 15 g; Cholesterol 179 mg; Sodium 149 mg; Dietary Fiber 3 g

Sautéed Potatoes

PREP TIME: 20 MINUTES

COOKING TIME: 30 MINUTES

INGREDIENTS

6 small Yukon gold potatoes

6 fingerling potatoes

6 small red potatoes

10 green (spring) onions, cut into
½-inch (12-mm) lengths, including
tender green tops

1 tablespoon chopped fresh savory
or 1 teaspoon dried savory

5 tablespoons (2½ oz/75 g) unsalted
butter

¼ cup (2 fl oz/60 ml) vegetable oil

salt and ground pepper to taste

¼ cup (⅓ oz/10 g) chopped flat-leaf
(Italian) parsley, for garnish

PREP TIP: Immersing raw potato
slices in cold water rinses off some
of their natural starch and makes for
crisper sautéed potatoes.

This timeless dish is updated using a variety of potatoes for an
interesting mix of color and texture.

SERVES 6

✹ Have ready a large bowl of cold water. Peel the Yukon gold potatoes,
cut into slices ⅛ inch (3 mm) thick, and immediately drop into the water.
Cut but do not peel the remaining potatoes the same thickness and add
to the water. (The potatoes can be left in the water for up to 4 hours
before cooking.) Drain and pat dry with paper towels just before frying.

✹ In a bowl, toss the green onions with the savory. In a large, heavy
cast-iron frying pan over high heat, melt the butter with the vegetable oil.
When the foam subsides, add the potatoes in batches alternately with
the green onions, season with salt and pepper, and allow an even brown
crust to form on the bottom, 8–10 minutes. Using a metal spatula, turn
the potatoes over, shaking the pan to redistribute the potatoes. If necessary, add more oil and adjust the heat to prevent burning. Continue
cooking until browned on the bottom, about 5 minutes. Reduce the heat
to medium-low, cover, and cook until the potatoes are almost tender,
about 10 minutes. Uncover, raise the heat to medium-high, and carefully
turn often until the potatoes are cooked through, about 5 minutes longer.
Season with salt and pepper, sprinkle with parsley, and serve.

NUTRITIONAL ANALYSIS PER SERVING: Calories 374 (Kilojoules 1,571); Protein 5 g;
Carbohydrates 46 g; Total Fat 19 g; Saturated Fat 7 g; Cholesterol 26 mg; Sodium 25 mg;
Dietary Fiber 5 g

Saucisson en Croûte

PREP TIME: 35 MINUTES, PLUS
2 HOURS FOR CHILLING

COOKING TIME: 1½ HOURS

INGREDIENTS

1 good-quality garlic sausage, about
2 lb (1 kg), 12 inches (30 cm) long
and 2 inches (5 cm) in diameter

½ head garlic, unpeeled

2 cups (16 fl oz/500 ml) full-bodied
red wine

PASTRY CRUST

3 cups (15 oz/470 g) all-purpose
(plain) flour

1 teaspoon dried fines herbes (parsley,
tarragon, chives, and chervil)

½ teaspoon salt

1 cup (8 oz/250 g) chilled unsalted
butter, cut into tablespoons

1 egg

6–8 tablespoons (3–4 fl oz/90–125 ml)
ice water

1 egg lightly beaten with 1 tablespoon
water for egg wash

MUSTARD SAUCE

1 tablespoon light brown sugar

2 teaspoons balsamic vinegar

1 teaspoon lemon juice

½ cup (4 oz/125 g) whole-grain
Dijon mustard

⅓ cup (2½ oz/75 g) smooth Dijon
mustard

1 small clove garlic, minced with a
pinch of salt

watercress sprigs

SERVES 6

✿ Using a knife tip, prick the sausage in 5 or 6 places, and place in a large nonaluminum frying pan over high heat. Add the garlic, wine, and cold water to cover. Cover, bring to a boil, reduce the heat to low, uncover, and simmer until the sausage is cooked, about 45 minutes. Drain and immediately place the sausage on a baking sheet lined with paper towels. Straighten it, set a second baking sheet on top, and weight with food cans. Let cool completely. Wrap and refrigerate until needed.

✿ To make the pastry crust, in a bowl, stir together the flour, fines herbes, and salt. Add the butter and, using a pastry blender, cut it in until the mixture resembles coarse meal. In a small bowl, using a fork, beat together 1 egg and 2 tablespoons of the ice water. Make a well in the flour mixture. Add the egg mixture and 2 more tablespoons ice water. Using the fork, mix lightly, adding more ice water as needed until the mixture holds together. Pat into a ball, wrap in plastic wrap, and refrigerate for 1 hour.

✿ Have ready the egg wash. Line a baking sheet with parchment (baking) paper. On a lightly floured work surface, roll out the pastry into an 8-by-16-inch (20-by-40-cm) rectangle. Place the sausage in the center and trim the pastry to allow an overlap of about ½ inch (12 mm) on all sides when the sausage is wrapped. Lift the long sides, brush the edges with water, then wrap the sausage, pressing the seam firmly to seal. Fold up the ends, brush the edges with water, then press to seal. Brush all the seams with egg wash. Transfer the wrapped sausage to the prepared baking sheet. Brush the entire pastry with egg wash. Cut out attractive shapes from the pastry scraps and use to decorate. Cut a few steam vents in the top, then again brush the entire pastry with egg wash. Refrigerate, uncovered, for 1 hour. Preheat an oven to 375°F (190°C).

✿ Bake until the pastry is golden brown and a knife inserted through a vent into the sausage comes out hot to the touch, about 45 minutes. Check after 25 minutes; if browning too fast, reduce to 350°F (180°C).

✿ To make the mustard sauce, in a small bowl, whisk together the brown sugar, vinegar, and lemon juice. Whisk in the mustards and garlic.

✿ Transfer the sausage to a platter and garnish with the watercress. Cut into thick slices. Pass the mustard sauce.

NUTRITIONAL ANALYSIS PER SERVING: Calories 1,075 (Kilojoules 4,515); Protein 31 g; Carbohydrates 62 g; Total Fat 74 g; Saturated Fat 35 g; Cholesterol 255 mg; Sodium 2,600 mg; Dietary Fiber 3 g

Raspberry Corn Muffins

PREP TIME: 20 MINUTES

COOKING TIME: 20 MINUTES

INGREDIENTS

¼ cup (2 oz/60 g) unsalted butter

2 eggs, beaten

1½ cups (12 fl oz/375 ml) buttermilk

1½ cups (7½ oz/235 g) stone-ground yellow cornmeal

½ cup (2½ oz/75 g) all-purpose (plain) flour

2 tablespoons sugar

2 teaspoons baking powder

I teaspoon salt

½ teaspoon baking soda (bicarbonate of soda)

grated zest of I orange

I cup (4 oz/125 g) raspberries

2 tablespoons raspberry preserves

Fresh raspberries and sweet preserves fill the center of this light corn muffin, adding a surprise to every mouthful. They are a wonderful treat and a great addition to an afternoon tea tray.

MAKES 12 MUFFINS

❀ Preheat an oven to 450°F (230°C). Generously grease 12 muffin cups with solid vegetable shortening or line them with foil or paper liners.

❀ In a small saucepan over low heat, melt the butter. Remove from the heat and let cool. In a small bowl, whisk the eggs until frothy, then whisk in the buttermilk. Set aside.

❀ In a sieve placed over a bowl, combine the cornmeal, flour, sugar, baking powder, salt, and baking soda. Shake the sieve to pass the mixture through. Add the orange zest and stir to mix. Make a well in the center. Whisk the cooled butter into the egg mixture, then pour into the well. Using a fork, mix just until the dry ingredients are moistened. The batter will look lumpy.

❀ Spoon the batter into the prepared muffin cups, filling each half full. Sprinkle a few raspberries into each cup, and then top with a dab of the raspberry preserves, dividing evenly. Spoon in the remaining batter, filling each cup about two-thirds full.

❀ Bake until light brown on top, firm to the touch, and the edges have pulled away from the sides of the cups, 15–20 minutes. Remove from the oven, invert onto a rack, and serve at once.

NUTRITIONAL ANALYSIS PER MUFFIN: Calories 182 (Kilojoules 764); Protein 4 g; Carbohydrates 24 g; Total Fat 8 g; Saturated Fat 3 g; Cholesterol 43 mg; Sodium 344 mg; Dietary Fiber 1 g

Spiced Applesauce Cake

PREP TIME: 20 MINUTES

COOKING TIME: 1¼ HOURS

INGREDIENTS

½ cup (2 oz/60 g) chopped walnuts

½ cup (4 oz/125 g) unsalted butter,
  at room temperature

1 cup (8 oz/250 g) granulated sugar

1 cup (9 oz/280 g) thick unsweetened
  applesauce

1 egg, beaten

1½ cups (7½ oz/235 g) all-purpose
  (plain) flour

4 teaspoons baking powder

1 teaspoon ground cinnamon

½ teaspoon salt

½ teaspoon ground nutmeg

¼ teaspoon ground cloves

¼ teaspoon ground allspice

OPTIONAL BROWN-BUTTER ICING
½ cup (4 oz/125 g) unsalted butter

3 cups (12 oz/375 g) confectioners'
  (icing) sugar

2 teaspoons vanilla extract (essence)

about 1 tablespoon heavy (double)
  cream

MAKE-AHEAD TIP: Bake this cake
in advance, if you like. Wrapped in
plastic wrap, it will keep at room
temperature for up to 2 days or in
the freezer for up to 2 months.

Plain slices of this cake are a perfect addition to any casual brunch buffet. When the occasion calls for something a little fancier, top it with the simple-to-make brown-butter icing. Its intriguing, slightly nutty flavor pairs wonderfully with the subtly spicy cake.

MAKES 1 LOAF; SERVES 12

❈ Preheat an oven to 375°F (190°C). Butter and flour a 9-by-5-by-3-inch (23-by-13-by-7.5-cm) loaf pan and tap out the excess flour.

❈ Spread the walnuts on a baking sheet and toast in the oven until they begin to color and are fragrant, 5–7 minutes. Remove from the oven and transfer to a small bowl to cool.

❈ In a large bowl, beat together the butter and granulated sugar until light and fluffy. Add the applesauce and egg and mix well.

❈ In a bowl, sift together the flour, baking powder, cinnamon, salt, nutmeg, cloves, and allspice. Add ¼ cup (1½ oz/45 g) of the flour mixture to the nuts and stir to coat. Add the remaining flour mixture to the applesauce mixture and stir until thoroughly combined. Fold in the walnuts. Pour into the prepared pan. Bake until a toothpick inserted into the center comes out clean, about 1 hour and 10 minutes.

❈ Meanwhile, make the icing, if desired: In a small saucepan over medium-high heat, melt the butter and continue to cook until it is the color of a brown paper bag, about 4 minutes. Do not allow it to burn. Remove from the heat and beat in the confectioners' sugar until smooth. Add the vanilla and enough cream to form a spreadable mixture.

❈ Transfer the cake to a rack and let cool in the pan for 10–15 minutes. If serving the cake plain, turn out onto the rack and let cool completely. If serving with the icing, set the warm cake on a rack over a plate or pan. Pour the icing over the top, letting it drip down the sides. Let stand until set, 20–25 minutes. Cut into slices and serve.

NUTRITIONAL ANALYSIS PER SERVING: Calories 258 (Kilojoules 1,084); Protein 3 g; Carbohydrates 37 g; Total Fat 12 g; Saturated Fat 5 g; Cholesterol 39 mg; Sodium 267 mg; Dietary Fiber 1 g

Old-fashioned Pecan Sticky Buns

PREP TIME: 45 MINUTES,
PLUS 9 HOURS FOR RISING

COOKING TIME: 35 MINUTES

INGREDIENTS

5 teaspoons (2 packages) active
dry yeast

2¼ cups (18 fl oz/560 ml) lukewarm
water (105°F/40°C)

1 teaspoon plus ½ cup (4 oz/125 g)
granulated sugar

8 cups (2½ lb/1.25 kg) all-purpose
(plain) flour

1 tablespoon salt

2 tablespoons unsalted butter, melted
and cooled

2 eggs, lightly beaten

GLAZE
½ cup (4 oz/125 g) unsalted butter,
plus ½ cup (4 oz/125 g), melted

2¼ cups (1 lb/500 g) firmly packed
light brown sugar

2 tablespoons dark corn syrup

pinch of salt

½ teaspoon vanilla extract (essence)

⅓–½ cup (3–4 fl oz/80–125 ml)
heavy (double) cream

about 2½ cups (10 oz/315 g)
coarsely chopped pecans, lightly
toasted in a 350°F (180°C) oven
for 5–7 minutes

MAKES 2½ DOZEN BUNS

❀ In a small bowl, sprinkle the yeast over ¼ cup (2 fl oz/60 ml) of the water, stir in the 1 teaspoon sugar, and let stand until foamy, about 5 minutes. In a large bowl, combine the remaining 2 cups (16 fl oz/500 ml) water, the ½ cup (4 oz/125 g) sugar, and 4 cups (1¼ lb/625 g) of the flour. Beat with a stand mixer fitted with the whisk attachment or a wooden spoon until smooth, about 5 minutes. Add the yeast mixture and beat for about 2 minutes. Add the salt, melted butter, eggs, and the remaining 4 cups (1¼ lb/625 g) flour and beat until smooth and elastic, 6–8 minutes. The dough will be sticky. Transfer to a very large bowl and slip a large plastic bag over the top, tucking the open ends under the bowl and leaving plenty of air space. Refrigerate overnight.

❀ The next day, make the glaze: In a small saucepan over medium heat, melt the ½ cup (4 oz/125 g) butter and stir in 1 cup (7 oz/220 g) of the brown sugar, the corn syrup, and the salt until the sugar dissolves, about 3 minutes. Remove from the heat and stir in the vanilla. In a small bowl, stir together the remaining 1¼ cups (9 oz/280 g) brown sugar and enough cream to form a spreadable mixture.

❀ Generously grease 2 or 3 rimmed baking sheets with solid vegetable shortening. Spread the butter-sugar mixture evenly over the prepared pans, then scatter about 2 tablespoons of the pecans over the top.

❀ Divide the dough in half. On a well-floured work surface, roll out one-half into a 12-by-15-inch (30-by-38-cm) rectangle. Generously brush the top with the melted butter. Spread on half of the cream-sugar mixture and sprinkle with half of the remaining pecans. Beginning with a long side, roll up the dough and pinch the seam securely closed. Cut into slices 1 inch (2.5 cm) thick and arrange, cut sides down, on the prepared baking sheets. Repeat with the remaining dough. Lightly cover with dampened kitchen towels and let rise until doubled, 45–50 minutes. Preheat the oven to 400°F (200°C).

❀ Bake for 10 minutes, then reduce the temperature to 350°F (180°C) and continue to bake, rotating the pans after 15 minutes to ensure even baking, until browned, 20–25 minutes longer. Immediately invert the pans onto racks. Let stand for 5 minutes to set the caramel, then lift off the pans. Let cool for at least 15 minutes before serving.

NUTRITIONAL ANALYSIS PER BUN: Calories 363 (Kilojoules 1,525); Protein 5 g; Carbohydrates 51 g; Total Fat 16 g; Saturated Fat 6 g; Cholesterol 37 mg; Sodium 253 mg; Dietary Fiber 2 g

Apricot-Glazed Pear Tart

PREP TIME: 20 MINUTES, PLUS
  20 MINUTES FOR THAWING

COOKING TIME: 50 MINUTES

INGREDIENTS

1 sheet (8 oz/250 g) frozen puff
  pastry, thawed at room temperature for 20 minutes

1 egg lightly beaten with 1 tablespoon
  water for egg wash

2 large, firm but ripe Bartlett
  (Williams') pears, about 9 oz
  (280 g) each

juice of 1 lemon

about 1½ tablespoons sugar

¼ cup (2½ oz/75 g) apricot jam

about 2½ teaspoons water

Although this classic tart takes only about 20 minutes to assemble, it looks like it came from a French pâtisserie. Serve with vanilla ice cream or yogurt cheese, if desired.

SERVES 6

❀ Preheat an oven to 400°F (200°C).

❀ On a floured work surface, roll out the puff pastry into a 12-by-6-inch (30-by-15-cm) rectangle. Using a pastry wheel, trim off a strip ¼ inch (6 mm) wide from each side. Using a pastry brush dipped in the egg wash, dampen the edges of the rectangle. Then return the strips to the edges, using them to form a rim around the rectangle. Brush the entire pastry with the egg wash. Transfer the pastry to an ungreased baking sheet.

❀ Peel, halve, and core the pears. Cut into lengthwise slices about ⅜ inch (1 cm) thick and immediately roll in the lemon juice to prevent discoloring.

❀ Sprinkle the pastry with about 1 teaspoon of the sugar or more to taste. Arrange the pear slices on the pastry, overlapping them in an attractive design. Sprinkle the pears with the remaining sugar. Bake for 15 minutes.

❀ Meanwhile, in a small saucepan over medium heat, melt the jam with enough water to thin to a brushing consistency. Remove from the heat and pass through a sieve placed over a small bowl to remove the fruit pieces; discard the pieces.

❀ Using a pastry brush, lightly brush the tops of the pears with the melted jam. Continue to bake, glazing the pears about every 10 minutes, until the pears are tender when pierced with the point of a knife and the crust is browned on the edges, 25–35 minutes. The baking time depends upon the ripeness of the pears and the thickness of the slices.

❀ Transfer to a rack and brush once again with the glaze. Let cool completely before serving.

NUTRITIONAL ANALYSIS PER SERVING: Calories 330 (Kilojoules 1,386); Protein 5 g; Carbohydrates 42 g; Total Fat 17 g; Saturated Fat 2 g; Cholesterol 35 mg; Sodium 117 mg; Dietary Fiber 3 g

Black and White Doughnut Holes

PREP TIME: 20 MINUTES, PLUS 2 HOURS FOR CHILLING

COOKING TIME: 45 MINUTES

INGREDIENTS

3½ cups (17½ oz/545 g) all-purpose (plain) flour, plus more as needed

1½ teaspoons baking powder

½ teaspoon baking soda (bicarbonate of soda)

¼ teaspoon ground nutmeg

pinch of ground mace

pinch of ground cardamom

pinch of salt

2 eggs

1 cup (8 oz/250 g) granulated sugar

1 cup (8 fl oz/250 ml) buttermilk

2 tablespoons unsalted butter, melted and slightly cooled

1 teaspoon lemon extract (essence)

vegetable oil for deep-frying

1½ cups (6 oz/185 g) confectioners' (icing) sugar

½ cup (1½ oz/45 g) Dutch-process cocoa powder

COOKING TIP: To check if the temperature of the oil is correct, fry 1 doughnut hole until golden brown, drain, and then break it open. If the oil is too hot, it will not be cooked on the inside; if the oil is not hot enough, the hole will be grease soaked.

For light-as-a-feather doughnut holes, keep all the ingredients as cold as possible before frying them. If you decide to make doughnuts rather than just the holes, cook them for 5–7 minutes. This recipe will make about 3 dozen doughnuts.

MAKES 9 DOZEN DOUGHNUT HOLES

✸ In a large bowl, sift the 3½ cups (17½ oz/545 g) flour. Then sift the flour again with the baking powder, baking soda, nutmeg, mace, cardamom, and salt.

✸ In a bowl, using an electric mixer set on medium speed, beat the eggs until frothy. Gradually add the granulated sugar, beating until light and lemon colored, about 4 minutes. Add the buttermilk, melted butter, and lemon extract and mix well. Pour the egg mixture into the center of the flour mixture and mix thoroughly. The dough will be very soft; add an additional sprinkle of flour if necessary to form a soft dough. (For light doughnuts, do not add any more flour than necessary.)

✸ Dust a work surface generously with flour. Scrape the dough onto the surface and dust the top with flour. Roll out the dough about ⅓ inch (9 mm) thick. Dip the center removable part of a doughnut cutter into a side dish of extra flour and cut out holes. Using an icing spatula, lift the holes onto an ungreased baking sheet. Cover with plastic wrap and refrigerate for at least 2 hours or for up to 1 day.

✸ To fry the doughnuts, in a deep-fat fryer or a deep saucepan, pour in oil to a depth of 3 inches (7.5 cm) and heat to 380°F (193°C) on a deep-frying thermometer, or until a doughnut hole dropped into the oil turns golden within about 2 minutes. Working in small batches, slip the doughnut holes into the oil and fry until golden brown, about 2 minutes. Using a skimmer or slotted spoon, transfer to paper towels to drain.

✸ Sift 1 cup (4 oz/125 g) of the confectioners' sugar into a paper bag. Sift together the remaining ½ cup (2 oz/60 g) confectioners' sugar with the cocoa into another bag. Just before serving, shake half of the doughnut holes in the bag with the plain sugar and the other half with the cocoa-sugar mixture. Arrange on a platter and serve.

NUTRITIONAL ANALYSIS PER PIECE: Calories 42 (Kilojoules 176); Protein 1 g; Carbohydrates 7 g; Total Fat 1 g; Saturated Fat 0 g; Cholesterol 5 mg; Sodium 20 mg; Dietary Fiber 0 g

English Scones

PREP TIME: 15 MINUTES

COOKING TIME: 10 MINUTES

INGREDIENTS

2 cups (10 oz/315 g) all-purpose
(plain) flour

2 teaspoons cream of tartar

1 teaspoon baking soda (bicarbonate
of soda)

1 teaspoon sugar

½ teaspoon salt

4 tablespoons (2 oz/60 g) unsalted
butter, chilled and cut into pieces

¾ cup (6 fl oz/180 ml) milk

Serve these fine scones with strawberry jam or a berry butter. If you like, add no more than ½ cup (3 oz/90 g) chopped plumped dried apricots, whole raisins, chopped crystallized ginger, or semisweet (plain) chocolate morsels to the dough just before it is kneaded. Fresh blueberries, dried cranberries, or chopped walnuts or pecans, again no more than ½ cup (2 oz/60 g), are also good additions.

MAKES 8–10 SCONES

❀ Preheat an oven to 450°F (230°C). Lightly grease a baking sheet with solid vegetable shortening.

❀ In a food processor, combine the flour, cream of tartar, baking soda, sugar, and salt. Pulse to combine. Add the butter and use on-off pulses until the mixture resembles coarse meal. Transfer to a bowl.

❀ Alternatively, in a bowl, stir together the dry ingredients. Then, using a pastry blender, cut in the butter until the mixture resembles coarse meal.

❀ Make a well in the center of the flour mixture and pour in the milk. Using a fork, mix together until a soft elastic dough forms.

❀ Turn out the dough onto a lightly floured work surface and knead 5 or 6 times until the dough is smooth. Roll out about ¼ inch (2 cm) thick. Using a scallop-edged cookie cutter 3 inches (7.5 cm) in diameter, cut out rounds. Transfer to the prepared baking sheet.

❀ Bake the scones until they rise and are golden brown on top, about 10 minutes. Serve hot.

NUTRITIONAL ANALYSIS PER SCONE: Calories 183 (Kilojoules 769); Protein 4 g; Carbohydrates 27 g; Total Fat 7 g; Saturated Fat 4 g; Cholesterol 17 mg; Sodium 280 mg; Dietary Fiber 1 g

Plum Upside-Down Cake

PREP TIME: 20 MINUTES

COOKING TIME: 1¼ HOURS

INGREDIENTS

½ cup (3½ oz/105 g) firmly packed
light brown sugar

1½ cups (12 oz/375 g) granulated
sugar

2 pinches of ground nutmeg

1 tablespoon unsalted butter, melted
and cooled

5 or 6 red plums, about 1½ lb (750 g),
pitted and sliced ½ inch (12 mm)
thick

½ cup (4 oz/125 g) unsalted butter,
at room temperature

2 eggs

1 tablespoon vanilla extract (essence)

1¾ cups (7 oz/220 g) sifted all-
purpose (plain) flour

1½ teaspoons baking powder

1 teaspoon ground cinnamon

1 teaspoon ground cardamom

¼ teaspoon salt

⅔ cup (5 fl oz/160 ml) milk

Cardamom adds an enticing taste to this cake, while the sugar-coated plums deliver a wonderful caramelized crown. The cake is delicious served warm or at room temperature. Whipped cream or vanilla ice cream is a good accompaniment.

SERVES 8–10

✱ Preheat an oven to 350°F (180°C). Coat the bottom and sides of a 9-inch (23-cm) round cake pan with 3-inch (7.5-cm) sides with nonstick cooking spray. Line the bottom of the pan with parchment (baking) paper.

✱ In a small bowl, stir together the brown sugar, ½ cup (4 oz/125 g) of the granulated sugar, and the nutmeg. Place the melted butter in another small bowl. Coat the plum slices first with the butter and then with the sugar mixture. Starting from the outside and working toward the center, arrange the plum slices in overlapping circles on the bottom of the prepared pan.

✱ In a food processor, combine the butter and the remaining 1 cup (8 oz/250 g) granulated sugar and process until fluffy. Add the eggs and vanilla and process until smooth. In a bowl, stir together the flour, baking powder, cinnamon, cardamom, and salt. Add half of the flour mixture to the processor and pulse 5 or 6 times to mix. Add the milk and pulse 5 or 6 times to combine. Add the remaining flour mixture and pulse just until mixed, 5 or 6 more times. Pour the batter over the plums, spreading it evenly.

✱ Bake until browned and a skewer inserted into the center comes out clean, 65–70 minutes. Transfer to a rack and let cool in the pan for 15 minutes. Run a knife around the inside edge of the pan and invert the cake onto a large serving plate. Peel off the parchment paper. Rearrange any plum slices that slip in the process. Serve warm or at room temperature.

NUTRITIONAL ANALYSIS PER SERVING: Calories 445 (Kilojoules 1,869); Protein 5 g; Carbohydrates 76 g; Total Fat 14 g; Saturated Fat 8 g; Cholesterol 81 mg; Sodium 175 mg; Dietary Fiber 2 g

Cheddar Cheese Buns

PREP TIME: 25 MINUTES, PLUS
1¾ HOURS FOR RISING

COOKING TIME: 30 MINUTES

INGREDIENTS

1½ cups (12 fl oz/375 ml) milk

⅓ cup (3 oz/90 g) plus 1 teaspoon
sugar

¼ cup (2 oz/60 g) unsalted butter

1 tablespoon salt

5 teaspoons (2 packages) active dry
yeast

½ cup (4 fl oz/125 ml) lukewarm
(105°F/40°C) water

1 egg, slightly beaten

1½ cups (6 oz/185 g) shredded sharp
cheddar cheese

about 6 cups (30 oz/940 g)
all-purpose (plain) flour

about 3 tablespoons butter, melted

1 yellow onion, finely chopped

These onion-topped cheese buns are delicious served with thin slices of ham slathered with mustard.

MAKES ABOUT 30 BUNS

❋ Pour the milk into a small saucepan over medium heat and warm until small bubbles appear along the edges of the pan. Remove from the heat, add the ⅓ cup (3 oz/90 g) sugar, the ¼ cup (2 oz/60 g) butter, and the salt; stir to dissolve the sugar. Let cool to lukewarm, about 105°F (40°C).

❋ Meanwhile, in a small bowl, sprinkle the yeast over the lukewarm water, stir in the 1 teaspoon sugar, and let stand until foamy, about 5 minutes. Transfer the yeast mixture to a large bowl and add the lukewarm milk mixture, egg, and cheese. Using a wooden spoon, beat until smooth. Add 3 cups (15 oz/470 g) of the flour and beat until well mixed. Continue adding the flour, about ½ cup (2½ oz/75 g) at a time and beating well after each addition, until the dough is smooth and comes away from the sides of the bowl, 10–12 minutes. (The dough can also be made with a stand mixer fitted with a dough hook; it will take 6–8 minutes.)

❋ Turn out the dough onto a floured board, cover with the bowl, and let rest for 5 minutes. Then knead until the dough is smooth and elastic and holds the imprint of a finger when poked, 7–9 minutes. Shape into a ball. Butter a clean bowl, place the ball in it, and turn to coat. Cover with a damp kitchen towel, set in a warm area away from drafts, and let the dough rise until doubled in bulk, about 1 hour.

❋ Grease 3 baking sheets with solid vegetable shortening or nonstick cooking spray. Using your hands, pinch off a tennis ball–sized piece of dough, shape into a ball, and place on the prepared sheet. Repeat until all the dough is shaped, spacing the buns about 2 inches (5 cm) apart. Flatten each bun with your fingers, brush the tops with the melted butter, and sprinkle about 1 teaspoon onion over each. Cover with a damp kitchen towel and let rise a second time until doubled in bulk, 30–40 minutes.

❋ Preheat an oven to 375°F (190°C).

❋ Bake until the tops are browned and the bottoms sound hollow when tapped, 25–30 minutes. Remove from the oven and serve warm.

NUTRITIONAL ANALYSIS PER BUN: Calories 175 (Kilojoules 735); Protein 5 g; Carbohydrates 25 g; Total Fat 6 g; Saturated Fat 3 g; Cholesterol 22 mg; Sodium 277 mg; Dietary Fiber 1 g

Blueberry Crumb Cake

PREP TIME: 20 MINUTES

COOKING TIME: 40 MINUTES

INGREDIENTS

2½ cups (7½ oz/230 g) sifted cake (soft-wheat) flour

2 cups (14 oz/440 g) firmly packed brown sugar

½ cup (4 oz/125 g) unsalted butter, chilled and cut into pieces

1 egg, beaten

2 teaspoons baking powder

1 teaspoon ground cinnamon

grated zest of 1 lemon

1 cup (8 fl oz/250 ml) milk

1½ cups (6 oz/185 g) blueberries

Plump blueberries top this cinnamon-and-lemon-scented cake, which tastes best the day it is baked. If you like, serve with vanilla-flavored whipped cream.

SERVES 8–10

❈ Preheat an oven to 350°F (180°C).

❈ Butter and flour a 9-by-13-inch (23-by-33-cm) cake pan and tap out the excess flour.

❈ In a food processor, combine 2 cups (6 oz/185 g) of the flour and the brown sugar and pulse to mix. Add the butter and process until crumbly, about 20 seconds. Transfer to a bowl; measure out ¾ cup (6 oz/185 g) and reserve for the topping.

❈ Add the egg to the remaining crumb mixture and mix well. In a small bowl, stir together the remaining ½ cup (1½ oz/45 g) flour, the baking powder, cinnamon, and lemon zest. Divide this mixture into 3 batches and stir it into the crumb mixture alternately with the milk in 2 batches, beginning and ending with the flour mixture. Pour the batter into the prepared pan.

❈ In a bowl, combine the reserved crumb mixture and the blueberries, toss well, and then scatter the mixture over the top of the cake. Bake until browned on top and a toothpick inserted into the center comes out clean, 30–40 minutes. Transfer to a rack and let cool for at least 20 minutes before cutting into squares to serve.

NUTRITIONAL ANALYSIS PER SERVING: Calories 385 (Kilojoules 1,617); Protein 4 g; Carbohydrates 67 g; Total Fat 12 g; Saturated Fat 7 g; Cholesterol 56 mg; Sodium 149 mg; Dietary Fiber 0 g

Dilled Batter Muffins

PREP TIME: 25 MINUTES, PLUS
1¼ HOURS FOR RISING

COOKING TIME: 25 MINUTES

INGREDIENTS

¾ cup (4 oz/120 g) all-purpose (plain) flour, plus 1½ cups (6 oz/185 g) sifted flour

2 tablespoons sugar

1 tablespoon grated yellow onion

1 tablespoon dill seeds

2½ teaspoons (1 package) active dry yeast

1 teaspoon salt

¼ teaspoon baking soda (bicarbonate of soda)

¼ cup (2 fl oz/60 ml) water

2 tablespoons unsalted butter

1 cup (8 oz/250 g) small-curd cottage cheese, at room temperature

1 egg, beaten

OPTIONAL COATING

½ cup (4 oz/125 g) unsalted butter, melted

¼ cup (2 oz/60 g) coarse salt

generous pinch of dill seeds

Rolling these moist miniature muffins in salted dill seeds gives them a crunchy coating and an extra dose of lively flavor.

MAKES 24 MINI MUFFINS

❁ In a bowl, stir together ¼ cup (1½ oz/45 g) of the flour, the sugar, onion, dill seeds, yeast, salt, and baking soda. In a small saucepan over low heat, warm the water and butter to 130°F (54°C). Add to the flour mixture and, using a stand mixer fitted with a paddle attachment, beat until smooth, about 2 minutes.

❁ Add the cottage cheese, egg, and the remaining ½ cup (2½ oz/75 g) flour. Beat on high speed until smooth and elastic, about 2 minutes. Add the 1½ cups (6 oz/185 g) sifted flour and again beat until smooth. Cover with plastic wrap and let rise in a warm place until doubled in bulk, about 45 minutes.

❁ Generously grease 24 mini muffin cups with solid vegetable shortening or nonstick spray. Using a wooden spoon, stir the batter down 25 times, then spoon it into the prepared muffin cups. Cover with a damp kitchen towel and let rise until doubled in bulk, about 30 minutes. Preheat an oven to 350°F (180°C).

❁ Bake until puffed and brown, 20–25 minutes.

❁ Meanwhile, make the coating, if using: Put the melted butter in a bowl. On a small plate, stir together the salt and dill seeds.

❁ When the muffins are ready, remove from the oven and immediately turn out onto a rack. If topping them, roll each hot muffin first in the melted butter, then dip the tops in the salt mixture. Serve at once.

NUTRITIONAL ANALYSIS PER MUFFIN: Calories 84 (Kilojoules 353); Protein 3 g; Carbohydrates 11 g; Total Fat 3 g; Saturated Fat 1 g; Cholesterol 13 mg; Sodium 151 mg; Dietary Fiber 0 g

Pumpkin-Date Bread

PREP TIME: 20 MINUTES

COOKING TIME: 1¼ HOURS

INGREDIENTS

1½ cups (6 oz/185 g) broken pecans

3 eggs

4 cups (2 lb/1 kg) sugar

1 can (29 oz/910 g) pumpkin purée

1 cup (8 fl oz/250 ml) vegetable oil

5 cups (25 oz/780 g) all-purpose
(plain) flour

1 tablespoon baking soda (bicarbonate of soda)

2 teaspoons ground cinnamon

1 teaspoon salt

½ teaspoon ground cloves

½ teaspoon ground nutmeg

2 cups (12 oz/375 g) pitted dates,
chopped

MAKE-AHEAD TIP: To store, wrap in
plastic wrap, then in a plastic bag,
and store at room temperature up to
3 days or freeze for up to 2 months.

The aromatic trio of cinnamon, cloves, and nutmeg enhances this rich-tasting quick bread. The recipe is generous: you'll end up with a loaf for brunch, one for the freezer, and one to give away.

MAKES 3 LOAVES; EACH LOAF SERVES 10

❈ Preheat an oven to 350°F (180°C). Butter and flour three 8½-by-4½-by-2½-inch (21.5-by-11.5-by-6-cm) loaf pans and tap out the excess flour.

❈ Spread the pecans on a baking sheet and toast until they begin to color and are aromatic, 5–7 minutes. Remove from the oven and transfer to a small bowl to cool.

❈ In a large bowl, using an electric mixer, beat the eggs until frothy. Gradually add the sugar and then the pumpkin purée, mixing well. Stir in the oil.

❈ In a bowl, sift together the flour, baking soda, cinnamon, salt, cloves, and nutmeg. Add the dates to the toasted pecans, then stir in ½ cup (2½ oz/75 g) of the flour mixture to coat. Stir the remaining flour mixture into the pumpkin mixture until thoroughly combined. Fold in the pecans and dates. Divide the batter evenly among the prepared loaf pans.

❈ Bake until the tops are browned, the loaves pull away from the sides of the pans, and a toothpick inserted into the center comes out clean, about 1 hour and 10 minutes. Transfer to racks and let cool in the pans for 10–15 minutes. Then turn out of the pans onto the racks and let cool completely before serving.

NUTRITIONAL ANALYSIS PER SERVING: Calories 360 (Kilojoules 1,512); Protein 4 g; Carbohydrates 61 g; Total Fat 12 g; Saturated Fat 2 g; Cholesterol 22 mg; Sodium 213 mg; Dietary Fiber 6 g

Fresh Strawberry Tart

PREP TIME: 40 MINUTES, PLUS
2 HOURS FOR CHILLING
PASTRY AND TART

COOKING TIME: 15 MINUTES

INGREDIENTS

PASTRY

3 cups (15 oz/470 g) all-purpose
(plain) flour

½ teaspoon salt

1 tablespoon sugar

1 cup (8 oz/250 g) chilled unsalted
butter, cut into small pieces

1 egg

1 teaspoon vanilla extract (essence)

6–8 tablespoons (3–4 fl oz/90–125 ml)
ice water

LEMON CURD

grated zest and juice of 4 large
lemons

1 cup (8 oz/250 g) sugar

½ cup (4 oz/125 g) unsalted butter

6 eggs

pinch of salt

½ cup (5 oz/155 g) red currant jelly

1½ tablespoons kirsch or water

3 cups (12 oz/375 g) strawberries,
stems removed

SERVES 8–10

❀ To make the pastry, in a bowl, stir together the flour, salt, and sugar. Add the butter and, using a pastry blender, cut it in until the mixture resembles coarse meal. In a small bowl, using a fork, beat the egg with the vanilla and 2 tablespoons of the ice water. Make a well in the flour mixture and pour in the egg and about 2 more tablespoons ice water. Mix lightly with the flour, adding more ice water as needed until the mixture holds together. Pat into a ball and wrap in plastic wrap. Refrigerate for 1 hour.

❀ Meanwhile, make the lemon curd: In a heavy nonaluminum saucepan over high heat, combine the lemon zest and juice, sugar, and butter. Stir until the sugar dissolves and the mixture comes to a boil, about 5 minutes. Remove from the heat. In a bowl, using an electric mixer set on high speed, beat together the eggs and salt until fluffy. Slowly beat in the hot lemon mixture. Return the mixture to the saucepan over low heat and cook, stirring constantly, until thick enough to coat the back of a spoon, about 4 minutes. Do not boil. Remove from the heat and transfer to a bowl. Cover with plastic wrap, pressing it directly onto the surface of the curd. Refrigerate until cool.

❀ On a floured work surface, roll out the pastry into a round about 13 inches (33 cm) in diameter. Transfer to an 11-inch (28-cm) tart pan with a removable bottom, trim the edges to make them flush with the pan rim, and prick the bottom in several places with a fork. Press a piece of aluminum foil, shiny side down, onto the crust, and freeze for about 30 minutes. Preheat an oven to 400°F (200°C).

❀ Bake the foil-lined pastry shell for 8 minutes. Remove the foil and continue to bake until lightly browned, about 6 minutes longer. Transfer to a rack and let cool completely.

❀ In a small saucepan over medium-high heat, melt the jelly with kirsch or water. Remove the sides from the tart pan, then slide the pastry shell off the base onto a serving plate. Spoon about 2 cups (16 fl oz/500 ml) of the lemon curd into the shell (reserve any remaining curd for another use). Arrange the strawberries on top, stem end down. Brush the strawberries with the melted jelly. Refrigerate until set, about 30 minutes, before serving.

NUTRITIONAL ANALYSIS PER SERVING: Calories 626 (Kilojoules 2,629); Protein 10 g; Carbohydrates 75 g; Total Fat 32 g; Saturated Fat 19 g; Cholesterol 214 mg; Sodium 193 mg; Dietary Fiber 2 g

Oatmeal Bran Muffins with Raisins and Almonds

PREP TIME: 20 MINUTES, PLUS
2 HOURS FOR CHILLING

COOKING TIME: 25 MINUTES

INGREDIENTS

½ cup (2½ oz/75 g) slivered
   blanched almonds

1 cup (2½ oz/75 g) 100% Bran®

1 cup (8 fl oz/250 ml) boiling water

½ cup (4 oz/125 g) unsalted butter,
   at room temperature

1½ cups (12 oz/375 g) sugar

2 cups (16 fl oz/500 ml) buttermilk

2 eggs, beaten

1 teaspoon almond extract (essence)

2 cups (10 oz/315 g) all-purpose
   (plain) flour

2 cups (5 oz/155 g) All-Bran®

½ cup (1½ oz/45 g) old-fashioned
   rolled oats

2½ teaspoons baking soda
   (bicarbonate of soda)

½ teaspoon salt

¾ cup (4 oz/125 g) golden raisins
   (sultanas)

MAKE-AHEAD TIP: The batter for
these muffins can be kept in the
refrigerator, ready for baking, for
up to 2 weeks.

The secret to the texture of these best-ever bran muffins is
using two kinds of bran cereal: 100% Bran® and All-Bran®.

MAKES 18 MUFFINS

❀ Preheat an oven to 350°F (180°C). Spread the almonds on a baking
sheet and toast until they begin to color and are fragrant, 5–7 minutes.
Remove from the oven and set aside.

❀ In a bowl, combine the 100% Bran and boiling water and let stand
until cool. Meanwhile, in a bowl, using an electric mixer set on high
speed, beat together the butter and sugar until light and fluffy, about 5
minutes. Add the buttermilk, eggs, almond extract, and the soaked bran,
stirring well after each addition. Then add the flour, All-Bran, rolled
oats, baking soda, and salt. Mix well. Fold in the raisins and almonds.
Cover tightly and refrigerate for at least 2 hours or for up to 2 weeks.

❀ Preheat an oven to 425°F (220°C). Generously grease 18 standard muffin cups with solid vegetable shortening or line them with paper liners.

❀ Spoon the batter into the prepared muffin cups, filling them full.
Bake until browned on top and the edges start to pull away from the
sides of the cups, about 25 minutes. Remove from the oven and turn
out onto a rack. Let cool for 10 minutes, then serve warm.

NUTRITIONAL ANALYSIS PER MUFFIN: Calories 297 (Kilojoules 1,247); Protein 6 g;
Carbohydrates 48 g; Total Fat 11 g; Saturated Fat 4 g; Cholesterol 38 mg; Sodium 367 mg;
Dietary Fiber 5 g

Honey-Glazed Baked Peaches

PREP TIME: 15 MINUTES

COOKING TIME: 30 MINUTES

INGREDIENTS

20 gingersnaps, each 1¾ inches
(4.5 cm) in diameter (about 4½ oz/
140 g total)

2 tablespoons unsalted butter,
at room temperature

grated zest of 1 orange

8 firm but ripe peaches, peeled,
pitted, and quartered

4 tablespoons (2 fl oz/60 ml) orange
juice

¼ cup (3 oz/90 g) honey

The honey glaze and cookie-crumb coating keep the peaches juicy. Vanilla-wafer crumbs flavored with 3 pinches of ground star anise can be substituted for the gingersnaps.

SERVES 8

❋ Preheat an oven to 375°F (190°C).

❋ In a food processor, combine the gingersnaps, butter, and orange zest. Process until crumbly. Set aside.

❋ Arrange the peach quarters, peeled side down, in a 2-qt (2-l) baking dish. Drizzle about 2 tablespoons of the orange juice over the peaches, then scatter the gingersnap crumbs over the top.

❋ Bake until the crumbs begin to brown, about 15 minutes.

❋ Meanwhile, in a small bowl, stir the remaining 2 tablespoons orange juice into the honey. Remove the baking dish from the oven, drizzle the honey mixture over the crumbs, and return the dish to the oven. Continue to bake until the peaches are tender but still hold their shape and the top is glazed, about 15 minutes longer.

❋ Serve hot directly from the baking dish.

NUTRITIONAL ANALYSIS PER SERVING: Calories 203 (Kilojoules 853); Protein 2 g; Carbohydrates 41 g; Total Fat 5 g; Saturated Fat 2 g; Cholesterol 8 mg; Sodium 105 mg; Dietary Fiber 3 g

Roasted Figs with Vanilla Crème Fraîche

PREP TIME: 20 MINUTES, PLUS
  3 HOURS FOR STEEPING
  SYRUP

COOKING TIME: 10 MINUTES

INGREDIENTS

1¼ cups (10 oz/315 g) sugar

1 cup (8 fl oz/250 ml) water

½ vanilla bean, split lengthwise

16 firm but ripe figs

1 tablespoon vanilla extract
  (essence), or to taste

1 cup (8 fl oz/250 ml) crème fraîche

8 fresh mint sprigs

Figs have two short seasons, one in summer and one in autumn, so act quickly when you see them in the market. For this easy dessert, choose perfect firm but ripe specimens, as they must hold their shape in the oven.

SERVES 8

❈ In a small saucepan over high heat, combine the sugar and water. Bring to a boil, stirring until the sugar dissolves. Add the vanilla bean and boil for 3 minutes, then remove from the heat. Cover and let stand at room temperature for at least 3 hours or for up to 24 hours. Remove and discard the vanilla bean. (The syrup can be stored in a tightly covered jar in the refrigerator for up to 2 weeks.)

❈ Preheat an oven to 500°F (260°C).

❈ Using a paring knife, and starting from the stem end, cut each fig into quarters about three-fourths of the way through, leaving the bottom intact. Place the figs in a single layer in a shallow baking dish. Pour about ⅔ cup (5 fl oz/160 ml) of the sugar syrup over and around the figs. Roast until the figs are tender yet hold their shape, 6–7 minutes. Just before the figs are ready, stir the vanilla extract into the crème fraîche.

❈ Remove the figs from the oven and transfer them to a platter. Fill the center of each fig with a dollop of the crème fraîche. Garnish with the mint sprigs and serve at once.

NUTRITIONAL ANALYSIS PER SERVING: Calories 327 (Kilojoules 1,373); Protein 2 g; Carbohydrates 56 g; Total Fat 11 g; Saturated Fat 7 g; Cholesterol 25 mg; Sodium 22 mg; Dietary Fiber 3 g

Caramel-Crusted Pineapple

PREP TIME: 10 MINUTES, PLUS
    2 HOURS FOR CHILLING

COOKING TIME: 5 MINUTES

INGREDIENTS

1 large pineapple

3 tablespoons kirsch

1½–2 cups (12–16 fl oz/375–500 ml)
    sour cream

⅔ cup (5 oz/155 g) firmly packed
    light brown sugar

The juxtaposition of chilled tart-sweet pineapple and rich sour cream under a caramelized crust is irresistible. Seedless green grapes can be prepared in the same way: use 1½ pounds (750 g).

SERVES 6

❋ Using a sharp knife, cut off the top of the pineapple just below the crown. Cut a slice ½ inch (12 mm) thick off the bottom. Place the pineapple upright and cut off the peel in vertical strips. Then, using the knife tip, cut out the round "eyes" on the pineapple sides. Cut crosswise into slices ½ inch (12 mm) thick, and cut the tough core out of the center of each slice. Arrange the slices slightly overlapping in an attractive shallow, nonaluminum, flameproof baking dish. They should fit snugly. Sprinkle the kirsch evenly over the top. Cover tightly and refrigerate for at least 2 hours or for up to 6 hours.

❋ Preheat a broiler (griller).

❋ Just before serving, spread the sour cream over the pineapple. Be sure the edges are completely covered and the layer of sour cream is about 1 inch (2.5 cm) thick. Evenly sprinkle the brown sugar over the sour cream. Immediately slip under the broiler about 3 inches (7.5 cm) from the heat source and broil (grill) until the brown sugar bubbles and is caramelized, about 4 minutes.

❋ Remove from the broiler and serve at once.

NUTRITIONAL ANALYSIS PER SERVING: Calories 362 (Kilojoules 1,520); Protein 3 g; Carbohydrates 56 g; Total Fat 15 g; Saturated Fat 9 g; Cholesterol 30 mg; Sodium 47 mg; Dietary Fiber 3 g

Citrus Compote

PREP TIME: 20 MINUTES,
PLUS 4 HOURS FOR
STEEPING AND CHILLING

INGREDIENTS

1 cup (8 oz/250 g) sugar

1 cup (8 fl oz/250 ml) water

6 whole cloves

2 large blood oranges

1 large white grapefruit

1 large pink grapefruit

2 large seedless oranges

6 kumquats, sliced

4 kiwifruits, peeled and diced

strawberries for garnish

For a less sweet compote, omit the sugar syrup and simply let the pared fruits macerate in their own juices for up to 6 hours.

SERVES 8

❀ In a small saucepan over high heat, combine the sugar and water. Bring to a boil, stirring until the sugar dissolves. Add the cloves and boil for 3 minutes, then remove from the heat. Cover and let stand at room temperature for at least 3 hours or for up to 24 hours. Remove the cloves and discard. Set the syrup aside. (The syrup can be stored in a tightly covered jar in the refrigerator for up to 2 weeks.)

❀ Using a sharp knife, cut a slice off the top and bottom of each blood orange to expose the fruit. Place each orange upright on a cutting board and thickly slice off the peel in strips, cutting around the contour of the fruit to expose the flesh. Holding each orange over a bowl, cut along either side of each section, letting the sections drop into the bowl. Squeeze the membrane portion of the fruit over the bowl to extract any juice, then discard the membrane along with any seeds. Repeat with the grapefruits and seedless oranges.

❀ Add the kumquats and kiwifruits to the bowl. Pour the clove-scented sugar syrup over the fruits, cover, and refrigerate until chilled, at least 1 hour or for up to 6 hours.

❀ Transfer the compote to a pretty glass bowl for a buffet, or spoon into old-style champagne glasses for individual portions. Serve chilled, garnished with the strawberries.

NUTRITIONAL ANALYSIS PER SERVING: Calories 212 (Kilojoules 890); Protein 2 g; Carbohydrates 54 g; Total Fat 0 g; Saturated Fat 0 g; Cholesterol 0 mg; Sodium 1 mg; Dietary Fiber 4 g

Apple-Cinnamon Bread Pudding

PREP TIME: 20 MINUTES, PLUS
6 HOURS FOR CHILLING

COOKING TIME: 1 HOUR

INGREDIENTS

1 loaf cinnamon raisin bread, 1 lb (500 g), sliced

8 eggs

2 cups (16 fl oz/500 ml) milk

1 cup (8 oz/250 g) sugar

1 tablespoon vanilla extract (essence)

4 Granny Smith apples, peeled, cored, and thinly sliced

1 cup (6 oz/185 g) golden raisins (sultanas) (optional)

1 tablespoon ground cinnamon

1 teaspoon ground nutmeg

3 tablespoons unsalted butter, cut into small pieces

1 cup (8 fl oz/250 ml) heavy (double) cream

This uncomplicated one-dish brunch entrée exemplifies comfort food at its best. Serve with Canadian bacon or thick slices of slab bacon on the side.

SERVES 6–8

❊ The day before serving, generously butter a deep 2-qt (2-l) baking dish. Line the bottom and sides of the dish with some of the bread slices, starting with the bottom and cutting and trimming the slices as needed. Leave a little edge of bread extending above the rim of the dish to support the pudding as it puffs.

❊ In a mixing bowl, whisk together the eggs, the milk, ½ cup (4 oz/125 g) of the sugar, and the vanilla. Pour half of the milk mixture into the bread-lined dish. Top with a layer of the apple slices and the raisins, if using, and then a layer of bread slices. Repeat until the dish is filled, ending with a layer of bread. Set the dish on a plate to catch any overflow, then pour the remaining milk mixture over the top. In a small bowl, stir together the cinnamon, nutmeg, and the remaining ½ cup (4 oz/125 g) sugar. Sprinkle the mixture over the top, then dot with the butter. Cover and refrigerate until the bread absorbs the liquid, 6–8 hours or for up to overnight.

❊ Preheat an oven to 350°F (180°C). Uncover the dish and place it in the oven. Bake until the top is browned and a knife inserted into the center comes out clean, 45 minutes–1 hour.

❊ In a bowl, using an electric mixer or a whisk, whip the cream just until it starts to thicken.

❊ Serve warm on individual plates. Spoon some of the cream over each serving.

NUTRITIONAL ANALYSIS PER SERVING: Calories 653 (Kilojoules 2,743); Protein 15 g; Carbohydrates 83 g; Total Fat 30 g; Saturated Fat 16 g; Cholesterol 315 mg; Sodium 374 mg; Dietary Fiber 4 g

Stewed Winter Compote

PREP TIME: 15 MINUTES

COOKING TIME: 35 MINUTES,
    PLUS 30 MINUTES FOR
    COOLING

INGREDIENTS

3 cups (24 fl oz/750 ml) water

1 cup (8 oz/250 g) sugar

pinch of salt

1⅓ cups (½ lb/250 g) pitted prunes

1⅓ cups (½ lb/250 g) dried golden figs

1⅓ cups (½ lb/250 g) raisins

1⅓ cups (½ lb/250 g) dried apricots

1 cup (¼ lb/125 g) dried cherries

grated zest of 1 lemon

grated zest of 1 orange

2 large, firm Bosc pears

1 large Granny Smith or other tart
    green apple

about 1 cup (8 fl oz/250 ml) good-
    quality brandy or port

MAKE-AHEAD TIP: The compote can
be made up to 2 weeks in advance
and stored in the refrigerator. Bring
to room temperature before serving.

In this delicious compote, dried fruits are slowly poached in a
citrus-flavored sugar syrup so that they retain their natural
shape, texture, and color. For the best flavor, let the fruits steep
in the syrup for several days before serving.

SERVES 6

✹ In a large, heavy nonaluminum saucepan over high heat, combine
the water, sugar, and salt and bring to a boil, stirring to dissolve the
sugar. Boil for 5 minutes, then reduce the heat to low and add the
prunes, figs, raisins, apricots, cherries, and lemon and orange zests.
Add enough hot water to cover the fruits by 2 inches (5 cm). Cover the
pan and simmer until the fruits are nearly plump and tender, about
20 minutes, adding more water if the pan begins to dry out.

✹ Meanwhile, halve and core the pears and the apple. Cut into thick
slices. When the dried fruits are nearly tender, add the pears and the
apple slices to the pan and continue to cook, covered, until tender, about
10 minutes longer. Transfer to a bowl. Taste and flavor the compote
with brandy or port. Cover and let cool for about 30 minutes before
serving. Serve warm or at room temperature.

NUTRITIONAL ANALYSIS PER SERVING: Calories 728 (Kilojoules 3,058); Protein 5 g;
Carbohydrates 165 g; Total Fat 1 g; Saturated Fat 0 g; Cholesterol 0 mg; Sodium 38 mg;
Dietary Fiber 13 g

Cinnamon-Baked Apples

PREP TIME: 25 MINUTES

COOKING TIME: 1½ HOURS

INGREDIENTS

8 large Rome Beauty apples

1¼ cups (10 oz/315 g) sugar

2 cups (16 fl oz/500 ml) heavy
  (double) cream

ground cinnamon

½ cup (4 fl oz/125 ml) water

Brushing the fruits with cream and then rolling them in sugar gives these baked apples an irresistible crisp crust. Many apple varieties are fine for baking, but the Rome Beauty holds its shape particularly well.

SERVES 8

❈ Preheat an oven to 300°F (150°C). Select a baking dish large enough for the apples to fit close together without touching.

❈ Working with 1 apple at a time, and using a sharp paring knife, remove the core from the stem end, cutting to within about ½ inch (12 mm) of the blossom end. Then, using the knife, slit just through the skin around the "waist" of each apple.

❈ Place the sugar in a small, shallow bowl. Pour ⅓ cup (3 fl oz/80 ml) of the cream into another small bowl. Dip a pastry brush into the bowl of cream and paint the surface of an apple. Immediately roll the apple in the sugar to coat completely. Place in the baking dish, stem end up, and sprinkle inside and out with cinnamon. Repeat with the remaining apples. Divide the sugar and cream remaining in the bowls among the apples, spooning them into the hollow cores. Pour the water into the bottom of the baking dish.

❈ Bake, basting every now and then with the pan liquid, until tender when pierced with a fork, about 1½ hours.

❈ Serve warm, at room temperature, or cold. Pass the remaining 1⅔ cups (13 fl oz/420 ml) cream in a pitcher at the table.

NUTRITIONAL ANALYSIS PER SERVING: Calories 466 (Kilojoules 1,957); Protein 2 g; Carbohydrates 69 g; Total Fat 23 g; Saturated Fat 14 g; Cholesterol 82 mg; Sodium 23 mg; Dietary Fiber 5 g

Fresh Melons with Yogurt Sauce

PREP TIME: 25 MINUTES, PLUS
1 HOUR FOR CHILLING

INGREDIENTS

2 cups (12 oz/375 g) peeled and
cubed Crenshaw melon

2 cups (12 oz/375 g) peeled and
cubed cantaloupe

2 cups (12 oz/375 g) peeled and
cubed honeydew melon

2 cups (12 oz/375 g) peeled and
cubed casaba melon

2 cups (12 oz/375 g) peeled and
cubed seedless watermelon

YOGURT SAUCE

1½ cups (12 oz/375 g) nonfat plain
yogurt

3 tablespoons honey, or to taste

3 tablespoons plus 2 teaspoons
minced crystallized ginger

Crystallized ginger adds a sweet-tart accent to the yogurt sauce, making it the perfect counterpoint to the colorful layers of cooling melon. For a spectacular and edible centerpiece, line the bottom of a large, footed clear glass punch bowl with fresh mint leaves, layer the variously colored melons on top, and refrigerate the whole affair until it's ice cold. Then, just before serving, spoon the yogurt sauce over the melon and garnish the edges with fresh mint bouquets.

SERVES 8

❀ The melons should be in 1-inch (2.5-cm) cubes. Place them in parfait glasses, alternating the different colors until the glasses are full. Cover and chill for at least 1 hour or for up to 3 hours.

❀ Meanwhile, make the yogurt sauce: Line a sieve with a damp kitchen towel and place over a small bowl. Spoon the yogurt into the lined sieve and refrigerate for at least 1 hour to drain. Transfer the yogurt to another small bowl and discard the accumulated liquid. Stir the 3 tablespoons each honey and ginger into the drained yogurt. Taste and adjust the sweetness with more honey, if needed.

❀ Spoon an equal amount of the yogurt sauce over the melon in each glass, and sprinkle with the remaining 2 teaspoons minced ginger, dividing evenly. Serve chilled.

NUTRITIONAL ANALYSIS PER SERVING: Calories 142 (Kilojoules 596); Protein 4 g; Carbohydrates 33 g; Total Fat 1 g; Saturated Fat 0 g; Cholesterol 1 mg; Sodium 56 mg; Dietary Fiber 2 g

Maple-Glazed Grapefruit

PREP TIME: 10 MINUTES

COOKING TIME: 10 MINUTES

INGREDIENTS

¾ cup (3 oz/90 g) chopped walnuts

3 large Ruby grapefruits, well chilled

⅔ cup (7 oz/220 g) Grade B maple
  syrup

1 tablespoon dark corn syrup

1 teaspoon vanilla extract (essence)

A layer of toasted walnuts coated with a sweet syrup forms a hot, crunchy glaze on the cold, juicy fruit. For the most intense maple flavor, use a Grade B maple syrup, which is darker and slightly thicker than the more costly Medium Amber or Fancy Grade syrups.

SERVES 6

❀ Preheat an oven to 350°F (180°C). Spread the walnuts on a baking sheet and toast until golden and fragrant, 5–7 minutes. Remove from the oven and let cool.

❀ Preheat a broiler (griller).

❀ Cut the grapefruits in half horizontally. Remove the center core and, using a small, sharp knife, cut along either side of each section to free it from the membrane. Place, cut sides up, on a broiler pan.

❀ In a small bowl, stir together the maple syrup, corn syrup, and vanilla. Sprinkle a generous tablespoon of walnuts over each grapefruit half, then drizzle with the syrup mixture, coating the nuts.

❀ Place under the broiler about 2 inches (5 cm) from the heat source and broil (grill), watching carefully to prevent burning, until the tops are browned and bubbly, 2–3 minutes.

❀ Transfer to individual plates and serve at once.

NUTRITIONAL ANALYSIS PER SERVING: Calories 235 (Kilojoules 987); Protein 3 g; Carbohydrates 39 g; Total Fat 9 g; Saturated Fat 1 g; Cholesterol 0 mg; Sodium 10 mg; Dietary Fiber 2 g

INGREDIENTS

APPLES

Whether served in fruit salads, cooked desserts, or baked goods, apples are among the most popular fruits for morning meals. Scores of different apple varieties are sold in food stores and farmers' markets, including those used in the recipes in this book. **Granny Smith** apples, native to Australia, are crisp, juicy, tart fruits with bright green skins. **Jonathans** have orange-streaked red skins and white, juicy, slightly tart flesh. **Macoun** apples, harvested in early autumn, have green skins blushed with red and slightly tart, crisp flesh. The **Rome Beauty**, popular for baking because it holds its large, round shape, has bright red skin sometimes striped with yellow, and a slightly tart flavor.

BERRIES

Fresh berries are one of the delights of the brunch table. Seek out each type in turn when it reaches its peak and is most plentiful; for cooked dishes, frozen berries are an acceptable substitute. Spherical, smooth-skinned blueberries (below) flourish from early June through midsummer; juicy red, purple-black, or golden **raspberries** are harvested throughout summer but are at their best at mid-season; and **straw-berries**, distinguished by their deep pink to red heart shapes, thrive from early spring to early summer. An exception to these typical berries are round, deep red, tart **cranberries**, which are grown primarily in wet, sandy coastal lands—or bogs—in the northeastern United States. They are available fresh from autumn through early winter and are sold frozen year-round, while their tangy, sweetened, bottled juice is also popular as a bright-colored, bracing addition to brunch-time beverages.

CANADIAN BACON

Far leaner than conventional streaky bacon, this form of cured and smoked pork is taken from the loin, which provides circular slices.

CHEESES

Various cheeses are used to add richness and distinctive flavor to eggs, breads, and other brunch dishes. Those that appear in the recipes in this book include **cheddar**, a semi-firm cheese ranging in taste from mild and mellow when fairly young to sharp and tangy when aged for 9 months or longer; **Comté**, a French cousin of Gruyère, less sweet in flavor than its Swiss relative; popular North American **cottage cheese**, a mild, creamy-tasting fresh curd cheese; **cream cheese**, a rich, slightly tangy fresh spread traditionally made from milk with a high butterfat content, preferably without the addition of emulsifiers; **feta**, a rich, tangy, crumbly white cheese made from sheep's milk; **Gruyère** (below), a variety of Swiss cheese famed for its sweet, nutty taste; **Parmesan**, an aged Italian cheese made from cow's milk with a sharp,

EQUIPMENT

CAST-IRON FRYING PAN
A good-quality cast-iron frying pan holds and transfers heat incomparably well. Shallow, sloped sides let moisture escape, ensuring even browning, and make it easy to turn ingredients in the pan. Ideal for frying eggs or meats for morning meals.

CREPE PAN
Made of black steel and relatively small in diameter, the ideal pan for making the ultrathin French pancakes known as crepes has shallow, sloping sides and a long handle. Crepe pan sizes are measured across the bottom.

GRIDDLE
Made of heavy, heat-conductive cast iron or aluminum, a griddle provides a large surface particularly convenient for cooking pancakes and French toast. Available in square or circular models designed to fit on one stove burner, or larger rectangular griddles that rest atop two burners.

salty flavor and firm texture ideal for grating, of which the finest is designated Parmigiano-Reggiano®; and **Swiss**, a generic term for cheeses typified by Switzerland's **Emmentaler**, a cow's milk cheese distinguished by its semi-firm texture, mild nutty flavor, and network of holes or "eyes."

CHILES

There are many varieties of chiles, in a wide range of shapes, sizes, colors, and heat levels. You'll find the best selection in Latin American, Asian, and farmers' markets. Those called for in this book include **fresh green chiles**, a generic term for the tiny, slender, hot **serrano** (below, bottom) variety of Mexico and the American Southwest or similar Asian chiles. **Jalapeños** (below, top), familiar small, fresh

green (or less often ripened red) chiles, have plump triangular bodies and thick, juicy,

slightly sweet, medium-hot to very hot flesh. They are also found smoke-dried under the name **chipotle chiles**, as well as crumbled into flakes. **Red pepper flakes**, sold in the spice section of food stores, are another way to add the heat of dried chiles to brunch dishes.

DRIED FRUIT

Drying concentrates the flavor of fruit and gives it a moist, chewy, texture. Dried fruit may be added to home-baked breads and other brunch treats. Those types used in this book include **apricots**, made from whole or halved fruits; **sour cherries**, pitted and kiln-dried with the addition of a little sugar; **figs**, of which the golden **Calimyrna** type are particularly prized for their sweet, nutty flavor; **raisins**, dried seedless dark or golden grapes; and **prunes**, dried plums with rich, fairly soft flesh.

EXTRACTS

Vanilla beans, almonds, and lemons are some of the common ingredients used to make extracts (essences). For the truest flavor, look for extracts labeled "pure" or "natural" except

when buying coconut extract, which is produced only in imitation form.

HERBS

Both fresh and dried herbs add flavor and fragrance to countless savory brunch dishes. Because the intensity of dried herbs dissipates over time, buy them in small quantities, keep them in airtight jars, and store in a cool, dry place. Before use, rub dried herbs between your fingertips to release more of their essential oils. To store fresh herbs, place the stem ends in a glass of water, or wrap whole sprigs in damp paper towels in a plastic bag; in either case, refrigerate them.

CHERVIL

A springtime herb with small leaves and a taste reminiscent of a mixture of parsley and anise. Use it fresh in salads and with vegetables or eggs.

CHIVES

Used most often as a garnish, chives have an onionlike flavor without the bite. Mild and

JELLY-ROLL PAN
This large, rectangular baking pan with a shallow rim, also known as a Swiss-roll pan, was designed for the large, thin cakes used to make jelly rolls. When made from heavy, durable aluminum, a jelly-roll pan can be used for just about anything that goes in the oven: cookies, biscuits—even roasts.

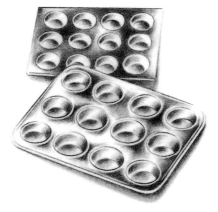

MUFFIN PANS
Used to bake muffins, cupcakes, popovers, tartlets, and mini quiches, these multicup pans come in three sizes: miniature (each cup holds about 1½ tablespoons); standard (½ cup/4 fl oz/125 ml); and oversized (¾ cup/6 fl oz/180 ml).

OMELET PAN
With its heavy, flat bottom and gently rounded sides, this pan is perfectly shaped to cook an omelet evenly and then roll it out easily and neatly onto a plate. The standard 8-inch (20-cm) size is perfect for cooking a 2- or 3-egg omelet.

sweet, they are at their best when fresh and raw, as drying and cooking diminish their flavor.

DILL

This feathery herb has a sprightly, almost sweet taste that is best appreciated when at its freshest, that is, when the leaves and stems are bright green. Small, crescent-shaped dill seeds, sold dried in the spice section of food stores, add a similar flavor.

OREGANO

Also known as wild marjoram, this pungent, spicy herb is used in all kinds of savory dishes and marries particularly well with tomatoes.

PARSLEY, FLAT-LEAF

Also known as Italian parsley, this variety of the widely popular fresh herb, native to southern Europe, has a more pronounced flavor than the common curly type, making it preferable as a seasoning.

ROSEMARY

Used either fresh or dried, this Mediterranean herb has a strong, aromatic flavor well suited to meats, poultry, seafood, and vegetables.

SAGE

This pungently flavored herb is enjoyed fresh or dried with poultry, lamb, veal, and most particularly pork. At brunch, it appears most often as a seasoning for sausages.

TARRAGON

With its distinctively sweet flavor reminiscent of anise, tarragon is used fresh to flavor eggs, poultry, vegetables, and salad dressings.

THYME

One of the most important culinary herbs of European kitchens, thyme has a light fragrance and subtle flavor and complements meats, poultry, and seafood, as well as vegetables and mild cheeses.

MAPLE SYRUP

The syrup of choice for pancakes and waffles, maple syrup is the boiled sap of the sugar maple tree, enjoyed for its rich, sweet taste and warm caramel color. Look for products labeled "pure" maple syrup, avoiding those that are diluted with cane or corn syrup. Pure maple syrups are graded by color and flavor, from Fancy Grade, which has a light amber hue and delicate taste, to those graded medium, dark, and B, which are progressively darker in color and stronger in flavor.

NUTS

The mellow taste and crunchy texture of nuts enhance many brunch-time breads, pancakes, and waffles. For the best selection, look in a specialty-food shop, health-food store, or the baking section of a food market. Some popular options used in this book include mellow, sweet **almonds**, commonly sold already skinned

EQUIPMENT

PASTRY WHEEL
Attached to a sturdy handle, this small, sharp-bladed wheel is used to cut rolled-out pie, pastry, and pasta doughs. For decorative crinkled edges, choose a fluted wheel.

TART PAN
The low, straight or fluted sides and removable bottom of this circular baking pan make it easy to unmold a filled tart or quiche. After baking and cooling, simply place the pan atop a level, raised object of smaller diameter, then gently loosen the rim of the pan and ease it down and away.

WAFFLE IRON
Whether designed with an electric heating element or for stove-top use, a waffle iron turns thin batters into golden, crisp waffles ready to top with syrup and melted butter. A waffle iron with a nonstick surface is easiest to cook with and clean. Follow manufacturer's instructions for your specific model.

(blanched) and cut into slivers; and brown-skinned, crinkly surfaced, rich **pecans**, usually sold as already shelled halves or smaller pieces.

ONIONS

All kinds of onions lend their flavor to savory brunch dishes. **Green onions**, also called spring onions or scallions, are a variety harvested immature, leaves and all. Both their green tops and white bulbs are appreciated for their mild but still pronounced onion taste. **Red (Spanish) onions** are a mild, sweet variety with purplish red skin and red-tinged white flesh. **Yellow onions**, the most common variety, have white flesh and a strong flavor. Their dry, yellowish brown skins make them easily recognizable.

PEARS

With their subtly sweet, juicy, highly aromatic flesh, pears make a wonderful fruit to enjoy raw or cooked at brunch. Some of the most common varieties are the **Anjou**, noted for its spicy flavor and smooth texture; and the **Bartlett (Williams')**, which has a mild flavor and fine texture. **Bosc pears** have a slightly grainy texture and remain crisp and firm when ripe.

POTATOES

The most commonly served vegetable at morning meals, potatoes come in many varieties, distinguished by size, shape, the color and thickness of their skins, and the color and texture of their flesh. Large **baking potatoes**, also known as Idahos or russets, have thick brown skins and a white flesh that cooks to a dry, mealy texture. **Fingerling potatoes** (below), most often found in farmers' markets and specialty-food stores, are small, waxy potatoes in slender, fingerlike shapes. **Red potatoes** are generally small and waxy, with white flesh and red skins. The **Yukon gold** is a small-to-medium-sized boiling potato with a fine-textured flesh, golden hue, and rich, buttery flavor. Popular in farmers' markets,

Yukon golds are also found with increasing frequency in well-stocked food stores.

VINEGARS

Though the name literally means "sour wine," vinegar is made from a variety of alcoholic ingredients including wine, beer, hard cider, and grain alcohol. The best vinegars ferment naturally and are then aged in wooden casks

SPICES

Aromatic seeds, berries, buds, roots, and barks are all used as spices and are indispensable flavor enhancers for both savory and sweet brunch dishes. Crushing spices releases their essential oils, so buy whole spices whenever possible and grind them as needed in an electric spice mill or in a mortar with a pestle. When only ground spices are available, buy them in small quantities and replenish your supply when their flavor diminishes.

ALLSPICE
This sweet Caribbean spice, sold ground or as whole dried berries, is named for its flavor, which resembles a blend of cinnamon, cloves, and nutmeg.

CARDAMOM
A sweet spice favored in Scandinavian, German, and Russian baked goods. The small, round seeds are enclosed in a pod that is easily split open to remove them for grinding.

CAYENNE PEPPER
Prized for its heat and bright red color, this powder is ground from the dried cayenne chile.

CINNAMON
One of the most popular spices for baking, cinnamon is made from the fine inner skin of the bark of the fragrant cinnamon tree. Cinnamon sticks, cut from the bark of the upper branches, are relatively low in

to develop their intense, complex flavors. **Balsamic vinegar** is made from reduced grape juice aged for many years in a succession of wooden barrels. The resulting vinegar is thick, syrupy, and intensely flavored. **White wine vinegar,** like all wine vinegars, reflects the character of the particular wine from which it was made.

flavor. Ground cinnamon is made from the lower, older bark and has a more potent taste.

CLOVES
These dried flower buds of an evergreen tree native to Southeast Asia have a rich, highly aromatic flavor. Use them whole or ground in both savory and sweet recipes.

MACE
Delicate and almost lacy in appearance, this red skin of the nutmeg shell carries subtle hints of that spice. Ground mace is sold in the spice section of most markets; mace flakes, also known as blades, are found in some Caribbean and Asian markets.

NUTMEG
This popular baking spice is ground from the hard fruit pit of the nutmeg tree. For the best flavor, grate nutmeg as needed.

PAPRIKA
Available in sweet, mild, and hot forms, this powdered spice is derived from the dried paprika pepper. Hungarian paprika is considered the best quality, but milder Spanish paprika may also be used.

INDEX

ACKNOWLEDGMENTS

The publishers would like to thank the following people and associations for their generous assistance and support in producing this book: Desne Border, Linda Bouchard, Ken DellaPenta, Hill Nutrition Associates, Cecily Upton

The following kindly lent props for photography: Fillamento, Williams-Sonoma, and Pottery Barn, San Francisco, CA. The photographer would also like to thank Chromeworks and ProCamera, San Francisco, CA, and FUJI film for their generous support of this project. Special acknowledgment goes to Daniel Yearwood for the beautiful backgrounds and surface treatments.

The author wishes to acknowledge with special thanks to Shpresa Lee for Oatmeal Bran Muffins with Raisins and Almonds; Penny Lawrence for Spinach and Feta Quiche; Carolyn Buster for Apple-Cinnamon Bread Pudding; Dorothy Burkholder for Dilled Batter Muffins; Opal Schrock, aka Mom, for Black and White Doughnut Holes; and Steven Schmidt for Cinnamon-Baked Apples.